Creating the Creation Caching Website

By Paul F. Taylor

Just Six Days Publishing

Published in the USA by J6D Publications, 5035 Spirit Lake Hwy, Toutle, WA 98649

shop@justsixdays.com

http://www.justsixdays.com

ISBN: 978-1523650125

Created with CreateSpace.com

Contents

Introduction

This is an unusual sort of book for me. My books are mostly Christian non-fiction; theological works on issues to do with creation, exegesis and apologetics. What am I doing with a book about web development?

In fact, I have been developing websites for about 20 years - since the web was in its infancy. I have seen web technologies come and go. I have seen killer apps launched, which have then faded. And, alongside the ministry that I have operated, I have always tended to do a few web development projects.

Indeed, before being in full time ministry, I used to train people in web technologies. In particular, I got used to using PHP and MySQL, and began to recommend these as the best backend technologies available.

Because these technologies were open source, many of the apps developed with them began to be open source. It was a thrill to be able to use other people's work, with no embarrassment, knowing that they had made them available for precisely that purpose. My own back contributions tended to be less spectacular, but they were available, nevertheless. I can recall the thrill

of producing extensions for the Dreamweaver software, and seeing people download them. One educational website carried an article of mine for years, explaining how to set up your own test web server. Indeed, it might even still be out there, though, if it is, it is now well out of date.

Wordpress

One of the most exciting of these open source applications was Wordpress. This was an entire content management system, built entirely out of PHP and MySQL. It was like being given a ladder to climb on. Wordpress was versatile enough to be able to be styled with themes, and adapted with plugins. There were lots of these available, but gradually I found that I could add to these myself, and began learning the craft of producing my own plugins and themes.

Prayer

There are Christians involved in web development. Many churches have such skilled people. But perhaps such people are not always as spiritually mature as they should be. It upsets me when I see churches using pirated software. And there is no need to use pirated technologies. It seems to me that the open source community is an admirable community, for Christians to get involved in. When I worked in a major Christian ministry in Florida, successive web developers were expert in the use of such technologies - especially with Wordpress.

But web development can be frustrating. Many is the time that I find myself wasting time, looking for a bug in my coding, and then suddenly being caught up short. I can't find the bug, because I haven't prayed.

Please do not think that I am advocating prayer as the magic solution for bad coding. All I am saying is that whatever job we are doing, it should be bathed in prayer.

Before I start the plan for a website, it should be bathed in prayer. Before, during, and after I have put together tricky coding in PHP, there should have been prayer. Whatever we do, should be done to the glory of God, yet so often, those of us designing websites forget this fact.

The Creation Caching website came about by prayer, and would never have happened without prayer.

Origin

While I was working for Creation Today, a supporter, who had discovered that I was interested in Geocaching™, drew my attention to the Earth Cache site. This set of educational, virtual caches did not involve the discovery of a physical cache. Instead, when the appropriate coordinates had been reached, one or two questions had to be answered. These questions were educational in nature, and usually concerned the geology of the area. As one might expect, the geological education provided was almost entirely evolutionary. Our supporter asked if I knew of an alternative, creationist caching site. I did not.

Periodically, I would scour the internet to see if any such site had been produced. Gradually, I realized that, if such a site were to happen, I would have to make it myself.

So, I started to look for plugins, that would enable caches to be created. However, still no such plugins appeared to be available. Over a period of several months, I realized that, if any such plugin were to happen, I would have to create it.

So, I launched a Github repository, and bought a book (see Appendix 1), and started to build my plugin. I did it a bit at a time, experimenting all the way. At first, I thought that other people would start to add ideas. But no such help was forthcoming. Nevertheless, I used spare moments to build extra functions and routines, until I had something that worked.

Having built the plugin, although it needed refining and debugging, I realized that the Creation caching website was now a possibility. And my renewed interest in coding had caused me to look at the possibility of creating my own theme, especially after I came across the concept of starter themes.

And Now a Book

Once the site was finished, and tested, it occurred to me that a book might be of use. But first, let me tell you what this book is not. This book is not a textbook on how to build websites. I have recommended 2 such books in Appendix 1. This book is more of a travelog. I expect that the readers will already be familiar with the technologies that I am using. So this book is not a textbook; it is an example book. Those of you who know how to do the coding might be interested in how I actually utilized that coding for the Creation Caching website.

The code for all the themes and plugins that I have made can be found on Github. I keep links to these Github repositories at my web development site:

Oldcastleweb.com

Happy coding!

What Did I Want?

Before getting down to building the website, I had to decide what I wanted. I was familiar with the Geocaching website, but realized I would not be able to create everything that that site had in place. So, what were the minimum things that I could expect my site to do?

It seemed sensible that each Creation Cache should have a page of its own. Therefore, it would need to draw its information in a standard manner from a database. Most of the caching websites that I studied enabled users to download a file, containing the cache information. These files had either .loc or .gpx file extensions. It would be good to produce one of these for each cache. As I started the project, I had no idea what these files would be like, but I assumed that they were probably xml files. It turned out that I was correct.

Basic Technologies

Having decided that the caches required data to be stored in a database, my next task was to work out what technologies to use to deliver the required result. My choice of PHP and MySQL was easy, because they are the technologies that I understand the best.

The ultimate website was going to need to deliver HTML pages. I wanted those pages to be in HTML5, to take advantage of the latest techniques. But the pages would be built on the fly by PHP, again in its latest format. It would make sense to have the ability to use Javascript, in order to produce some client-side effects. Finally, the data from the pages would be stored in a MySQL database. In order to take advantage of the PHP coding language, your computer needs to be running a web server. Probably the easiest web server to use with PHP - and the one most often used on live websites - is Apache.

In order to use these technologies, it is important to have the basic elements installed on your computer. I am only reporting on what I did, and I use Windows computers. So I needed a web server on my computer, that would deliver pages on the fly, so I had to have PHP installed as well, as well as the Apache webserver. And, of course, I needed to install the MySQL database server. These technologies can all be installed separately, and manually, but there are a number of Windows compatible packages available out there. The one that I have been using is XAMPP.

XAMPP is downloaded (free, because it is open source) from www.apachefriends.org. Once you have downloaded the Windows version, you just need to install it. As it installs, it will warn you that, unlike other applications, it should not be installed in the Program Files folder. Instead, you should allow it to make its own xampp folder on the C: drive. You will notice that the latest version of XAMPP uses a database server called MariaDB, instead of MySQL. Don't worry about this; it is

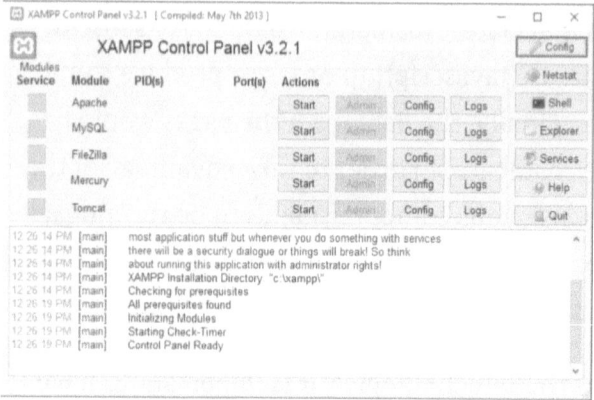 actually the same thing. MariaDB is an open source forked version of MySQL, made by the same team that actually created MySQL in the first place. So the applications that you make on your PC with MariaDB will work online with a MySQL server.

When you have installed XAMPP, you will have a control panel, with which to start Apache and MySQL. You do not need to start the other servers.

Before you start the services, you should note that, on Windows 10, you might have a problem with Apache. This is because Windows 10 automatically installs and starts Microsoft's own webserver, called Internet Information Server (IIS). Of course, this server might be useful - for example, if you are also wanting to develop asp.net applications. But IIS will be "listening" on the same port (port 80) as Apache, which is a conflict. You either need to permanently switch off IIS, or change either IIS or Apache to an alternative listening port. The best alternative is port 8080. In a browser, port 80 is served by http://localhost, or http://127.0.0.1. If you use port 8080, then you will have to use http://localhost:8080, or http://127.0.0.1:8080. It does not matter which you use, but make a decision and stick to it, because you will probably find it difficult to alter things later.

To find IIS, search in the Administrative tools of the Control Panel. Either stop this service permanently, or click configure. Under configure, find the port number and change to 8080.

Alternatively, change Apache. Click the config button in the XAMPP panel, to open up the Apache httpd.conf file in your favorite text editor (I use Notepad++). Search for LISTEN. You should find the line, with the code Listen 80. Change this to Listen 8080 and restart Apache.

I no longer do anything with asp.net, which I find an expensive technology. So, I have permanently stopped the IIS server, and left Apache on port 80.

In addition to this server, you need something to code your web applications with. I like to use Netbeans, which is an opensource IDE, and enables me to document all my new PHP functions etc.

Wordpress

Although, in theory, I could build my application from scratch, I see little point in doing this, when other people have produced excellent open source systems for me to use. For this reason, almost all my websites these days are built on the Wordpress content management system (CMS). My design for the Creation Caching site therefore involved new plugins and themes. I could have used an existing theme, but I decided this was the opportunity to build a new theme of my own. The Creation cache pages, however, are generated by a custom built plugin. The plugin creates a new custom post type, with its own custom taxonomy, and also the ability to produce the .gpx and .loc files. Other plugins used were those already created by others, perhaps with a little tweaking from me.

The whole Wordpress application is downloaded from wordpress.org. The zip file produced is extracted into a new subfolder, inside the htdocs folder inside the xampp folder. You normally need to create a new blank database. Any subfolder inside htdocs will be accessed through your browser as a subfolder of localhost. For example, if your subfolder inside htdocs is called myapp, you access it through the browser at http://localhost/myapp. The first time you do this should enable you to install the Wordpress system.

The Creation Cache Plugin

This chapter might well be of particular interest, as it involves making a new custom post type.

It was clear to begin with that the creation cache post type would need to store more information than a regular post. So, the first decision was where to store the extra information. One option would be to create a new table within the Wordpress database to store the new information. Clearly, this would give good control over what fields to use. However, new routines would need to be written to make sure that uninstalling the plugin would lead to the new table being deleted. My experience with other plugins has been that these routines are often not well written, or implemented, leaving bloated, useless, unused tables in the application.

Wordpress has an alternative ready-made system. It has a special postmeta table, for storing what is referred to as meta data. Each record in the postmeta table stores its own id number, plus the postid (indicating the post id record number) and whatever other information is being stored. This table is most often used by plugins, so I decided to use it myself for the extra data required, rather than making my own table.

Examining the .gpx File

The extra fields required would be those needed to create the .gpx files. So it seemed that I needed to open a file up, to

check what was inside. As I guessed, the .gpx file is really an
xml file, so it can be opened up in a text editor. As I said earlier,
my preferred text editor is Notepad++. When I opened the file,
Notepad++ did not recognize the xml language, so I used the
Language menu to force it to recognize the code as xml. The
code produced from a typical gpx file is shown below.

```
File MSHCC_2CUUF.gpx

01: <?xml version="1.0" encoding="utf-8"?>
02: <gpx
xmlns:xsi="http://www.w3.org/2001/XMLSchema-
instance"
xmlns:xsd="http://www.w3.org/2001/XMLSchema"
version="1.0" creator="Mount St Helens Creation
Center. All Rights Reserved.
http://www.mshcreationcenter.org"
xsi:schemaLocation="http://www.topografix.com/GPX/
1/0 http://www.topografix.com/GPX/1/0/gpx.xsd
http://www.groundspeak.com/cache/1/0
http://www.groundspeak.com/cache/1/0/cache.xsd"
xmlns="http://www.topografix.com/GPX/1/0">
03:    <name>Creation Cache listing from
mshcreationcenter.org</name>
04:    <desc>This is an individual cache generated
from mshcreationcenter.org</desc>
05:    <author>Account "pftaylor61" From
mshcreationcenter.org</author>
06:    <email>info@mshcreationcenter.org</email>
07:    <url>http://www.mshcreationcenter.org</url>
08:    <urlname>Creation Caching - the treasure
hunting bug with a biblical and scientific
perspective</urlname>
09:    <time>1451179367</time>
10:    <keywords>cache, geocache,
creationcache</keywords>
11:    <bounds minlat="30.35236403" minlon="-
87.29761565" maxlat="30.35236403" maxlon="-
87.29761565" />
12:    <wpt lat="30.35236403" lon="-87.29761565">
13:    <time>2015-12-27</time>
```

```
14:      <name>MSHCC_2CUUF</name>
15:      <desc>Trench Trail by pftaylor61, Unknown
Cache (0.5/0.5)</desc>
16:
<url>http://localhost/creationcaching/creationcache
/trench-trail/</url>
17:      <urlname>Trench Trail</urlname>
18:      <sym>Creation Cache Found</sym>
19:      <type>Creation Cache|Unknown Cache</type>
20:          <groundspeak:cache  id="75"
available="True"  archived="False"
xmlns:groundspeak="http://www.groundspeak.com/cache
/1/0">
21:              <groundspeak:name>Trench
Trail</groundspeak:name>
22:
<groundspeak:placed_by>pftaylor61</groundspeak:plac
ed_by>
23:
<groundspeak:owner>pftaylor61</groundspeak:owner>
24:              <groundspeak:type><a
href="http://localhost/creationcaching/cachetype/vi
rt/" rel="tag">Virtual</a> Cache</groundspeak:type>
25:
<groundspeak:container>Unknown</groundspeak:contain
er>
26:
<groundspeak:difficulty>0.5</groundspeak:difficul
ty>
27:
<groundspeak:terrain>0.5</groundspeak:terrain>
28:
<groundspeak:country>USA</groundspeak:country>
29:
<groundspeak:state>FL</groundspeak:state>
30:          <groundspeak:short_description
html="True">The  &lt;strong&gt;Trench
Trail&lt;/strong&gt; is a half-mile walk between
Fort Barrancas and Advance Redoubt in the Navy Air
Station at Pensacola, Florida. Park at either of
the forts, and walk along the Trench Trail, which
is well signposted from both. The trail runs
alongside a gun trench built between the two forts,
as an extra defensive structure between the
forts.</groundspeak:short_description>
```

```
  31:              <groundspeak:long_description
html="True">&lt;p&gt;The  &lt;strong&gt;Trench
Trail&lt;/strong&gt; is a half-mile walk between
&lt;strong&gt;Fort Barrancas&lt;/strong&gt; and
&lt;strong&gt;Advance Redoubt&lt;/strong&gt; in the
Navy Air Station at Pensacola, Florida. Park at
either of the forts, and walk along the Trench
Trail, which is well signposted from both. The
trail runs alongside a gun trench built between the
two forts, as an extra defensive structure between
the forts.&lt;/p&gt;
  32: &lt;p&gt;As this cache is on the Navy Base,
it can only be a virtual cache; it would not be
allowed to place a traditional cache, for obvious
security reasons. The coordinates are easy to
follow, leading you to an information board, that
provides the answer to the question below. Answer
the question to claim your cache! I do not need an
email &amp;#8211; I will trust you to be honest.
After all, if you cheat, you are only cheating
yourself &amp;#8211; there are no prizes!&lt;/p&gt;
  33: &lt;p&gt;Entry to the Navy Base is through a
security checkpoint. You must show ID at the
entrance to the base, and you may be required to
submit to a vehicle search.&lt;/p&gt;
  34: &lt;h3&gt;Question&lt;/h3&gt;
  35: &lt;p&gt;Which regiment strengthened the
Trench Trail in the Winter of 1864-65?&lt;/p&gt;
  36: &lt;p&gt;While you are here, try to find the
&lt;a
href=&quot;http://localhost/creationcaching/creatio
ncache/advance-redoubt/&quot;&gt;Advance
Redoubt&lt;/a&gt; cache as well.&lt;/p&gt;
  37: </groundspeak:long_description>
  38:         <groundspeak:encoded_hints>
  39:         </groundspeak:encoded_hints>
  40:         <groundspeak:travelbugs />
  41:      </groundspeak:cache>
  42:    </wpt>
  43: </gpx>
```

When you look at all these elements, you will realize that a field for every xml tag is not necessary. Some tags contain standard information. Others appear to repeat information.

The various tags containing the word groundspeak appear, because groundspeak is the company that owns the Geocaching™ website and system. Although I could have written my own new specification, I decided for portability t would be easier to use that of groundspeak. I notice that some other open source caching systems also do this.

Eventually, I realized that I would need the following extra fields:

Creation Cache Code (an id number), Creation Cache Owner, Date Created, Difficulty, Terrain, Longitude, Latitude, Country, State/Province, and a Short Description. The Long Description would be held in the normal post format. I would also need to add a taxonomy - called Cache Type.

Before proceeding, it might be necessary to have a look at the (shorter) .loc file type. This is not as useful in caching as the .gpx file, but is sometimes used for waymarks, so it needs checking.

File MSHCC_2CUUF.loc

```
01: <?xml version="1.0" encoding="UTF-8"?>
02: <loc version="1.0" src="Groundspeak">
03: <waypoint>
04: <name id="MSHCC_2CUUF"><![CDATA[Trench Trail
by pftaylor61]]>
05: </name>
06: <coord lat="30.35236403" lon="-87.29761565"/>
07: <type>Geocache</type>
```

```
08:    <link   text="Cache
Details">http://localhost/creationcaching/creationc
ache/trench-trail/</link>
09:    <difficulty>0.5</difficulty>
10:    <terrain>0.5</terrain>
11:    <container></container>
12:    </waypoint></loc>
```

It can be seen that this file type does not require extra fields. The fields designed above can be used.

Setting Up the Plugin

It is not the task of this book to give you every piece of information on how to create plugins. I strongly recommend that you get hold of the book *Professional Wordpress Plugin Development* by Williams, Richard and Tadlock. This will give you the reasons behind all the steps. I am simply going to record what I did. In order to find the reasons why I did what I did, please refer to the book suggested, or a similar textbook.

I made a subfolder in the plugins folder of the application. Then I created the main plugin file. This particular plugin ended up needing several files, but there is a minimum of one control file needed with the same name as the folder.

The info lines of my main file were as follows:

```
File ocws-creationcache.php

001:  <?php
002:
003:  /*
004:
005:  Plugin Name: OCWS Creation Cache
006:  Plugin URI:
http://oldcastleweb.com/pws/plugins
```

```
007:
008: Description: This plugin creates a new page
type, called creationcache, which displays Creation
caches - a version of the geocache system. The
plugin has been produced by <a
href="http://www.oldcastleweb.com"
target="_blank">Old Castle Web Solutions</a>.<br
/><br /> The actual name of the caches can be
changed from Creation Caches to any other name that
you choose, by ediiting a simple configuration file.
In order to explain the game of creation caching,
there is an extensive backend information page,
which appears where a settings page would normally
be. This page explains to the site owner how they
can go about administering a Creation Cache section
on their Wordpress website.<br /><br />I am quite
satisfied with the way the system works so far.
However, I would welcome reports to the website
above.
009:
010: Version: 1.0.0
011: Author: Paul Taylor
012: Author URI:
http://oldcastleweb.com/pws/about
013: License: GPL2
014: GitHub Plugin URI:
https://github.com/pftaylor61/ocws-creationcache
015: GitHub Branch:    master
016:
017: */
```

The reasons for lines 14 and 15 are these. I took a decision, which I will explain below, that prevented me from registering this plugin with the standard Wordpress plugin repository. In any case, it seemed easier to host the code on Github. There is a Wordpress plugin, found exclusively on Github, called the Github Updater. Adding this plugin to the site enables updates to be made to Github-hosed plugins, provided two lines are added to the plugin code, as shown at lines 14 and 15.

Having placed this minimum code in the plugin file, and saving it, I found the plugin in the Wordpress backend, and activated it. The next few lines in the file simply give the licensing information.

```
019: /* Copyright 2015  Paul Taylor  (email :
info@oldcastleweb.com)
020:
021:
022:
023:      This program is free software; you can
redistribute it and/or modify
024:      it under the terms of the GNU General
Public License, version 2, as
025:       published by the Free Software
Foundation.
026:
027:      This program is distributed in the hope
that it will be useful,
028:      but WITHOUT ANY WARRANTY; without even
the implied warranty of
029:       MERCHANTABILITY or FITNESS FOR A
PARTICULAR PURPOSE.  See the
030:      GNU General Public License for more
details.
031:
032:      You should have received a copy of the
GNU General Public License
033:      along with this program; if not, write
to the Free Software
034:      Foundation, Inc., 51 Franklin St, Fifth
Floor, Boston, MA  02110-1301  USA
035:
036: */
```

The next job was that I knew I was going to split up the plugin's operations into a number of files. Originally, I knew I would need 3 files. In the end, I have defined four. I will explain these below the code.

```
038: $ocwscc_base_dir = dirname( __FILE__ );
039: $ocwscc_base_url = plugins_url( '', __FILE__
);
040:
041:
042:
043:
044: // The configuration file can be amended, as
the user sees fit
045:   require_once($ocwscc_base_dir."ocws-
creationcache-config.php");
046:
047: // let's get the functions loaded and the
initialization done
048: // This applies the plugin's configuration
file
049:   require_once($ocwscc_base_dir."/ocws-
creationcache-categoryimages.php");
050:
require_once($ocwscc_base_dir."/functions.php");
051:
require_once($ocwscc_base_dir."/Initialize.php");
```

The file functions.php contains the majority of the functions needed. However, I decided to put a few functions in a file called initialize.php. These are the functions which get everything built up to begin with.

The file ocws-creationcache-config.php is the file that prevented this plugin's registration with Wordpress. I thought that not everyone would want to call their caches "Creation Caches". So I placed configuration for all the terms required in that file, so that the user could change everything. Wordpress wanted this altering, so that a user admin panel would enable the changes, but I preferred the whole plugin to be owned by the user. The full listing for the config file is given below:

File ocws-creationcache-config.php

```
01: <?php
02: /**
03: * This is the plugin's configuration file
04: * Users can amend this file, so that their
caches can have their own names
05: **/
06:
07: // These are the main definitions
08:
09: /* These constants can be amended for
personal choice */
10: /*
=====================================================
*/
11:
12: define("CCNAME_SG","Creation Cache"); //
Change 'Creation Cache' for the singular term for
your caches
13: define("CCNAME_PL","Creation Caches"); //
Change 'Creation Caches' for the plural term for
your caches
14: define("CCNAME_ACT","Creation Caching"); //
Change 'Creation Caching' for the activity present
participle for your caches
15: define("CCSLUG","creationcache"); // Change
creationcache for the slug used for your caches
16: define("CCVERSION","1.0.0"); // Set the
version number
17: define("CC_LOGO16","celticcross16x16.png");
// Set this to the 16x16 logo that you want. Copy
this logo into the plugin's image subfolder
18: define("CC_LOGO80","celticcross80x80.png");
// Set this to the 80x80 logo that you want. Copy
this logo into the plugin's image subfolder
19: define("CC_PRFX","OCWSCC_"); // This is the
prefix for the Creation Cache code
20:
21: /* only edit the lines below if you know what
you are doing */
22: /*
23:
24: $dash_url = get_bloginfo('url') . '/wp-
admin/options-general.php?page=ocws_creationcache';
```

```
25: $dash_info = "<p>The OCWS Creationcache
Plugin,  version  ".CCVERSION.",  will  display
".CCNAME_PL." and allow you to create, edit and
delete them. You can also download .gpx and .loc
files for your ".CCNAME_SG.".</p>";
  26:  $dash_info  .=  "<p>The  plugin's  <a
href=\"".$dash_url."\">information page</a> might
be helpful!</p>";
  27: define("CCDASH_INFO",$dash_info); // Set the
dashboard plugin info
  28:
  29: /* Other constants - DO NOT CHANGE!!! */
  30: /* ================================= */
  31:
  32: define("OCWSCC_BASE_DIR",dirname(__FILE__));
  33: define("OCWSCC_BASE_URL",plugins_url( '',
__FILE__ ));
  34: $cc_upload = wp_upload_dir();
  35: $cc_rpath = realpath($cc_upload['basedir']);
  36: $cc_upl_url = $cc_upload['baseurl'];
  37:  define("OCWSCC_GPX",
$cc_rpath."/ocwscc_gpx/");
  38:  define("OCWSCC_GPX_URL",
$cc_upl_url."/ocwscc_gpx/");
  39:
define("OCWSCC_EDITCONF",admin_url()."/plugin-
editor.php?file=ocws-creationcache%2Focws-
creationcache-config.php&plugin=ocws-
creationcache%2Focws-creationcache.php");
  40:
define("OCWSCC_IMAGE_PLACEHOLDER",OCWSCC_BASE_URL."
/images/placeholder.png")
  41: ?>
```

The file for category images came later, when I realized that
the category taxonomy for the Creation Cache custom post
type would look better, if each cache type could have a user-
defined image. So I put the functions required for this in a
separate file. The above code listing will also show that three
image files were needed, which I put in a subfolder of the
plugin, called "images".

The rest of the base file contains the action statements required, and I will cover these later. For now, it is time to move on to the initialize.php file.

Creation Cache Initialization

The first thing to notice is that in the main file, I had to make sure that the config file was called before this initialize.php file. That way, I could use constants defined in the config file.

Having analyzed what fields were required for the creation cache custom post type, it was time to define the post type. This started with the following lines:

File initialize.php

```
007: // Our custom post type function
008: function creationcache_posttype_init() {
009:
010:   // CPT Options
011:   $args = array(
012:           'labels' => array(
013:                   'name' => __( CCNAME_PL ,
CCSLUG),
014:                   'singular_name' => __(
CCNAME_SG , CCSLUG),
015:                   'add_new' => __( 'Add New',
CCSLUG ),
016:                   'add_new_item' => __( 'Add New
'.CCNAME_SG, CCSLUG ),
017:                   'edit_item' => __( 'Edit
'.CCNAME_SG, CCSLUG ),
018:                   'new_item' => __( 'New
'.CCNAME_SG, CCSLUG ),
019:                   'view_item' => __( 'View
'.CCNAME_SG, CCSLUG ),
020:                   'search_items' => __( 'Search
'.CCNAME_PL, CCSLUG ),
021:                   'not_found' => __( 'No
'.CCNAME_PL.' found', CCSLUG ),
022:                   'not_found_in_trash' => __(
'No '.CCNAME_PL.' found in Trash', CCSLUG ),
023:                   'parent_item_colon' => __(
'Parent '.CCNAME_SG.':', CCSLUG ),
```

```
024:                'menu_name' => __( CCNAME_PL,
CCSLUG ),
025:                ),
026:                'public' => true,
027:                'show_ui' => true,
028:                'capability_type' => 'post',
029:                'hierarchical' => false,
030:                'query_var' => true,
031:                'menu_icon'  =>
OCWSCC_BASE_URL.'/images/'.CC_LOGO16,
032:                'has_archive' => true,
033:                'rewrite' => array('slug' =>
CCSLUG),
034:                'supports' => array(
035:                   'title',
036:                   'editor',
037:                   'excerpt',
038:                   'trackbacks',
039:                   'custom-fields',
040:                   'comments',
041:                   'revisions',
042:                   'thumbnail',
043:                   'author',
044:                   'page-attributes',
045:                   ),
046:
047:             );
048:     register_post_type( CCSLUG, $args);
049:   add_filter('manage_edit-
'.CCSLUG.'_columns',
'add_new_creationcache_columns');
050:

add_action('manage_'.CCSLUG.'_posts_custom_column',
'manage_creationcache_columns', 10, 2);
051:   add_filter( 'manage_edit-
'.CCSLUG.'_sortable_columns',
'creationcache_sortable_columns' );
052:   /* Only run our customization on the
'edit.php' page in the admin. */
053:   add_action( 'load-edit.php',
'my_edit_creationcache_load' );
054:
055:
056: } // end function create_posttype
```

The reason for each of these arguments can be found in the book recommended in the previous chapter. Lines 48-53 are also laying down the necessities for further functions to be defined, which we will come to below. My next task was to define the taxonomy required. I wanted just one taxonomy - Cache Type - which is analogous to the Category for posts.

```
060:  // create a taxonomy based on cache-type
061:
062:  function cache_type_taxonomy() {
063:      register_taxonomy(
064:          'cachetype',
065:          CCSLUG,
066:          array(
067:              'hierarchical' => true,
068:              'label' => 'Cache Type',
069:              'query_var' => true,
070:              'rewrite' => array(
071:                  'slug' => 'cachetype',
072:                  'with_front' => false
073:              )
074:          )
075:      );
076:  }
```

Finally, all that was needed in this file was a function to create the creation cache pages, and the activation hook to make this work, when the plugin is activated.

```
079:  // Function used to automatically create
Creation Cache page.
080:  function create_creation_cache_pages()
081:      {
082:
083:      //post status and options
084:      $post = array(
085:          'comment_status' => 'open',
086:          'ping_status' => 'closed' ,
087:          'post_date' => date('Y-m-d H:i:s'),
```

```
088:              'post_name' => CCSLUG,
089:              'post_status' => 'publish' ,
090:              'post_title' => CCNAME_PL,
091:              'post_type' => 'page',
092:          );
093:          //insert page and save the id
094:          $newvalue = wp_insert_post( $post, false
);
095:          //save the id in the database
096:          update_option( 'ccpage', $newvalue );
097:
098:
099:     }
100:
101:   // // Activates function if plugin is
activated
102:   register_activation_hook(  __FILE__,
'create_creation_cache_pages');
```

The remaining code in the main file can now be given.

```
063: /* Initiation */
064:
065: // make the new directory
066:      if (!file_exists(OCWSCC_GPX)) {
067:          mkdir(OCWSCC_GPX, 0777, true);
068:          //echo OCWSCC_GPX;
069:      }
070:
071: // get the styles working
072: add_action( 'wp_enqueue_scripts',
'ocwscc_styles' );
073:
074: // Hooking up our function to theme setup
075: add_action( 'init',
'creationcache_posttype_init' );
076:
077: add_action( 'init', 'cache_type_taxonomy');
078:
079: // make an info page, where the settings
normally go
080:   add_action('admin_menu',
'ocwscc_admin_menu');
081:
082: $plugin = plugin_basename(__FILE__);
```

```
083:
084: add_filter("plugin_action_links_$plugin",
'ocws_creationcache_info_link' );
085:
086: // let's make a dashboard widget to report
my plugin
087: /* start dashboard widget code */
088: add_action( 'wp_dashboard_setup',
'ocwscc_dashboard_example_widgets' );
089:
090:
add_action('add_meta_boxes','ocwscc_mbe_create');
091: add_action('save_post',
'ocwscc_mbe_function_save');
092: add_filter( 'single_template',
'get_custom_post_type_template' );
093: add_filter( 'archive_template',
'get_custom_post_type_archtemplate' );
094:
095: // Add to admin_init function
096:
097:
098:
099: /* end dashboard widget code */
```

This code contains the hooks required to action the initialization functions. There are also calls that I added for a dashboard widget, which is not really necessary, and also for the various activities required by the functions.php file. The functions referenced in those code lines are contained in the next chapter.

OCWS Creationcache Plugin

The OCWS Creationcache Plugin. version 1.0.0. will display Creation Caches and allow you to create, edit and delete them. You can also download .gpx and .loc files for your Creation Cache.

The plugin's information page might be helpful!

Further information can be obtained from Oldcastle Web Services.

The Basic Plugin Functions

This chapter goes through the biggest file in the plugin; my functions.php file. The first job was to make sure that I could use special styles for the plugin. So I created a css file for the purpose, and the first part of the functions.php file is to enqueue this file.

```
006: // styles
007: function ocwscc_styles() {
008:   wp_enqueue_style( 'ocws-creationcache-
styles', OCWSCC_BASE_URL.'/ocws-creationcache-
styles.css' );
009: }
```

Randomized String

I then decided that I needed a function to create a randomized string. I was going to use this to create a unique ID indicator for each cache. So that function came next.

```
011: // function to create a random string
012: if (!function_exists('ocws_randomstring')) {
013: function ocws_randomstring($ocwsl,$ocseed) {
014:   $olength = $ocwsl;
015:   $ostring = "";
016:   $ocharacters =
"ABCDEFGHIJKLMNOPQRSTUVWXYZ0123456789"; // change to
whatever characters you want
017:   while ($olength > 0) {
018:     // echo $olength;
019:     $ostring .=
$ocharacters[mt_rand(0,strlen($ocharacters)-1)];
020:     $olength -= 1;
021:   }
022:   $ostring = $ocseed.$ostring;
023:   return $ostring;
024: } // end function ocws_randomstring
025: } // end if
```

This function enabled me to create a randomized string, containing capitals and numerals, with a total length of $ocws1 characters. I also wanted to add a prefix string to this, so that is referenced in the function as $ocseed. The function was used later in the file, in this way:

```
$ocwscc_ccname = ocws_randomstring(5,CC_PRFX);
```

Dashboard Widget

I thought it might be useful to have a dashboard widget, to give information about this complex plugin. This was achieved as follows:

```
027: /* This will create the dashboard widget */
028: function ocwscc_dashboard_example_widgets()
{
029:
030:   //create a custom dashboard widget
031:   wp_add_dashboard_widget(
'dashboard_custom_feed', 'OCWS Creationcache Plugin',
'ocwscc_dashboard_example_display' );
032:
033: }
034:
035: function ocwscc_dashboard_example_display()
036: {
037:          echo  "<img
src=\"".OCWSCC_BASE_URL."/images/".CC_LOGO80."\"
alt=\"Old Castle Web Services logo\" title=\"OCWS
logo\"  width=\"60\"  height=\"60\"
style=\"float:left;padding-right:10px;\" />\n";
038:   echo "<p>".CCDASH_INFO."</p>\n";
039:   echo "<hr style=\"align:center; width:80%\"
/>\n";
040:   echo "<p>Further information can be
obtained from <a
href=\"http://www.oldcastleweb.com\"
```

```
title=\"Oldcastle  Web  Services\"
target=\"_blank\">Oldcastle  Web
Services</a>.</p>\n";
  041: }
  042: /* end of dashboard widget functions */
```

This function links with the hook provided in the main file, as shown in the last chapter.

Line 31 above is the Wordpress function to make the Dashboard Widget. The content of the widget is then defined in the function from lines 35 through 42.

Meta Boxes

It would now be necessary to create the metaboxes needed on the admin UI page for the Creation Cache custom post type. This is very involved, and requires nearly 400 lines of code! Nevertheless, I will break it down bit by bit.

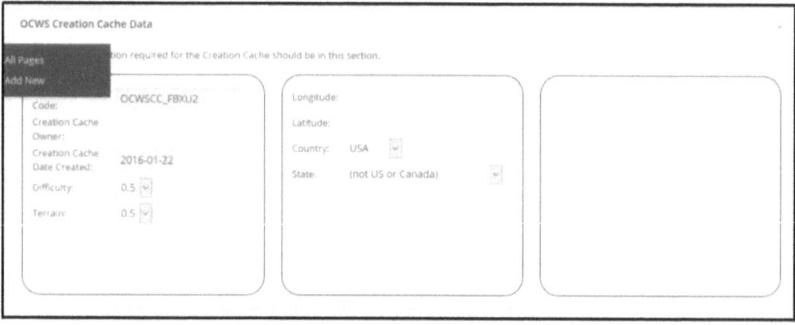

First, I decided to have two separate metaboxes. The first would contain most of the boxes needed. The second would contain a new editor box, to create the short description. The normal existing editor box would be used to create the main page content for the creation cache.

```
044: /* META BOXES CODE */
045: /* (I might not need the database functions
below) */
046: /* we need meta boxes */
047: function ocwscc_mbe_create() {
048:
049:    //create a custom meta box
050:    add_meta_box( 'ocwscc-meta', 'OCWS
'.CCNAME_SG.' Data', 'ocwscc_mbe_function', CCSLUG,
'normal', 'high' );
051:    add_meta_box( 'ocwscc-meta-shortdesc',
'OCWS '.CCNAME_SG.' Short Description',
'ocwscc_mbe_function_sd', CCSLUG, 'normal', 'high'
);
052:
053: }
```

The function ocwscc_mbe_function is very big. So I will have to explain it in bits. The first part of the function declares the variables which are to be saved in the postmeta table. But, of course, these values might already exist, so the function checks for them and loads their existing values. It is not necessary to put this in an if routine, because if the values don't exist, empty strings will be created, which will work fine for our purpose.

```
059: function ocwscc_mbe_function($post) {
060:    echo "<p>All the extra information
required for the ".CCNAME_SG." should be in this
section.</p>";
061:
062:    // let's see if any metadata values exist
063:    $ocwscc_ccname = get_post_meta( $post->ID,
'_ocwscc_ccname', true);
```

```
064:    $ocwscc_ccdate = get_post_meta( $post->ID,
'_ocwscc_ccdate', true);
065:    $ocwscc_cclon = get_post_meta( $post->ID,
'_ocwscc_cclon', true);
066:    $ocwscc_cclat = get_post_meta( $post->ID,
'_ocwscc_cclat', true);
067:    $ocwscc_gpname = get_post_meta( $post->ID,
'_ocwscc_gpname', true);
068:    $ocwscc_gpowner = get_post_meta( $post->ID,
'_ocwscc_gpowner', true);
069:    $ocwscc_gpdiff = get_post_meta( $post->ID,
'_ocwscc_gpdiff', true);
070:    $ocwscc_gpterr = get_post_meta( $post->ID,
'_ocwscc_gpterr', true);
071:    $ocwscc_gpcountry = get_post_meta( $post-
>ID, '_ocwscc_gpcountry', true);
072:    $ocwscc_gpstate = get_post_meta( $post->ID,
'_ocwscc_gpstate', true);
073:
074:    if ( $ocwscc_ccname == "") {
075:        $ocwscc_ccname =
ocws_randomstring(5,CC_PRFX);
076:        $ocwscc_ccdate = date('Y-m-d');
077:    }
```

The _ccname variable will only be empty, if no creation cache has already been made. Therefore, this is used as a test. If the value does not exist, then the variable is filled with the random string, and the date is stamped.

My first metabox then contains three tables. The first of these contains the elements for storing the Creation Cache Code, Owner, Date, Difficulty and Terrain.

```
085:    <table id="ocws_metaboxtable"
style="width:100%; border:0;">
086:    <tr>
087:    <td style="width:33%">
088:        <div  id="ocws_box_left"
style="border:solid 1px #000000; border-
```

```
radius:25px; padding:10px;
width:90%;float:left;min-height:270px;">
  089:          <table width="100%">
  090:              <tr><!-- Row 1 -->
  091:                  <td><?php echo CCNAME_SG."
Code:";?></td><!-- Col 1 -->
  092:                  <td><input type="text"
name="ocwscc_ccname" value="<?php echo
esc_attr($ocwscc_ccname); ?>" readonly /></td><!--
Col 2 -->
  093:              </tr>
  094:              <tr><!-- Row 2 -->
  095:                  <td><?php echo CCNAME_SG."
Owner:";?></td><!-- Col 1 -->
  096:                  <td><input type="text"
name="ocwscc_gpowner" value="<?php echo
esc_attr($ocwscc_gpowner); ?>" /></td><!-- Col 2
-->
  097:              </tr>
  098:              <tr><!-- Row 3 -->
  099:                  <td><?php echo CCNAME_SG." Date
Created:";?></td><!-- Col 1 -->
  100:                  <td><input type="text"
name="ocwscc_ccdate" value="<?php echo
esc_attr($ocwscc_ccdate); ?>" readonly /></td><!--
Col 2 -->
  101:              </tr>
  102:              <tr><!-- Row 4 -->
  103:                  <td>Difficulty:</td><!-- Col 1
-->
  104:                  <td><select
name="ocwscc_gpdiff">
  105:                      <option value="0.5" <?php
selected($ocwscc_gpdiff, 0.5); ?>>0.5</option>
  106:                      <option value="1.0" <?php
selected($ocwscc_gpdiff, 1.0); ?>>1.0</option>
  107:                      <option value="1.5" <?php
selected($ocwscc_gpdiff, 1.5); ?>>1.5</option>
  108:                      <option value="2.0" <?php
selected($ocwscc_gpdiff, 2.0); ?>>2.0</option>
  109:                      <option value="2.5" <?php
selected($ocwscc_gpdiff, 2.5); ?>>2.5</option>
  110:                      <option value="3.0" <?php
selected($ocwscc_gpdiff, 3.0); ?>>3.0</option>
  111:                      <option value="3.5" <?php
selected($ocwscc_gpdiff, 3.5); ?>>3.5</option>
```

```
112:                    <option value="4.0" <?php
selected($ocwscc_gpdiff, 4.0); ?>>4.0</option>
113:                    <option value="4.5" <?php
selected($ocwscc_gpdiff, 4.5); ?>>4.5</option>
114:                    <option value="5.0" <?php
selected($ocwscc_gpdiff, 5.0); ?>>5.0</option>
115:                    </select><!-- end select
ocwscc_gpdiff --></td><!-- Col 2 -->
116:            </tr>
117:            <tr><!-- Row 5 -->
118:                <td>Terrain:</td><!-- Col 1 -->
119:                <td><select
name="ocwscc_gpterr">
120:                    <option value="0.5" <?php
selected($ocwscc_gpterr, 0.5); ?>>0.5</option>
121:                    <option value="1.0" <?php
selected($ocwscc_gpterr, 1.0); ?>>1.0</option>
122:                    <option value="1.5" <?php
selected($ocwscc_gpterr, 1.5); ?>>1.5</option>
123:                    <option value="2.0" <?php
selected($ocwscc_gpterr, 2.0); ?>>2.0</option>
124:                    <option value="2.5" <?php
selected($ocwscc_gpterr, 2.5); ?>>2.5</option>
125:                    <option value="3.0" <?php
selected($ocwscc_gpterr, 3.0); ?>>3.0</option>
126:                    <option value="3.5" <?php
selected($ocwscc_gpterr, 3.5); ?>>3.5</option>
127:                    <option value="4.0" <?php
selected($ocwscc_gpterr, 4.0); ?>>4.0</option>
128:                    <option value="4.5" <?php
selected($ocwscc_gpterr, 4.5); ?>>4.5</option>
129:                    <option value="5.0" <?php
selected($ocwscc_gpterr, 5.0); ?>>5.0</option>
130:                    </select><!-- end select
ocwscc_gpterr --></td><!-- Col 2 -->
131:            </tr>
132:        </table>
133:
134:    </div><!-- end ocws_box_left -->
135:    </td>
```

So, there is a table within a table here. The initial table is started in line 85, but this code does not complete it. Inside the single table row, I added an inner table, to hold the data required. The difficulty and terrain values are defined by dropdown lists.

There is a huge dropdown in the second box, containing info for all the US states and Canadian provinces. I have only included part of that code, because I think the rest will be obvious.

```
136:        <td style="width:33%">
137:
138:     <div id="ocws_box_mid" style="border:solid
1px #000000; border-radius:25px; padding:10px;
width:90%; margin-left:auto; margin-right:auto;min-
height:270px;">
139:           <table width="100%">
140:              <tr><!-- Row 1 -->
141:                <td>Longitude:</td><!-- Col 1
-->
142:                   <td><input type="text"
name="ocwscc_cclon" value="<?php echo
esc_attr($ocwscc_cclon); ?>" /></td><!-- Col 2 -->
143:              </tr>
144:              <tr><!-- Row 2 -->
145:                <td>Latitude:</td><!-- Col 1
-->
146:                   <td><input type="text"
name="ocwscc_cclat" value="<?php echo
esc_attr($ocwscc_cclat); ?>" /></td><!-- Col 2 -->
147:              </tr>
148:              <tr><!-- Row 3 -->
149:                <td>Country:</td><!-- Col 1 -->
150:                       <td><select
name="ocwscc_gpcountry">
151:           <option value="USA" <?php
selected($ocwscc_gpcountry, 'USA'); ?>>USA</option>
152:           <option value="UK" <?php
selected($ocwscc_gpcountry, 'UK'); ?>>UK</option>
153:           <option value="Canada" <?php
selected($ocwscc_gpcountry, 'Canada');
?>>Canada</option>
154:
```

```
155:        </select><!-- end select
ocwscc_gpcountry --></td><!-- Col 2 -->
156:             </tr>
157:             <tr><!-- Row 4 -->
158:                 <td>State:</td><!-- Col 1 -->
159:                    <td><select
name="ocwscc_gpstate">
160:        <option value="n/a">(not US or
Canada)</option>
161:        <option value="AL" <?php
selected($ocwscc_gpstate,  'AL');
?>>Alabama</option>
162:        <option value="AK" <?php
selected($ocwscc_gpstate, 'AK'); ?>>Alaska</option>
163:        <option value="AZ" <?php
selected($ocwscc_gpstate,  'AZ');
?>>Arizona</option>
164:        <option value="AR" <?php
selected($ocwscc_gpstate,  'AR');
?>>Arkansas</option>
165:        <option value="CA" <?php
selected($ocwscc_gpstate,  'CA');
?>>California</option>
   —
212:        <option value="AB" <?php
selected($ocwscc_gpstate,  'AB');
?>>Alberta</option>
213:        <option value="BC" <?php
selected($ocwscc_gpstate,  'BC');  ?>>British
Columbia</option>
   —
225:        </select></td><!-- Col 2 -->
226:             </tr>
227:             </table>
228:
229:
230:     </div><!-- end ocws_box_mid -->
231:     </td>
```

The final box is designed to display a small map of the creation cache. The display requires using Google maps, and my special Google Maps function is listed later in this chapter.

```
232:     <td style="width:33%">
```

```
233:
234:          <div  id="ocws_box_right"
style="border:solid  1px  #000000;  border-
radius:25px;  padding:10px;
width:90%;float:right;text-align:center;min-
height:270px;">
235:      <?php
236:          if  (($ocwscc_cclon  !=  "")  &&
($ocwscc_cclat != "")) {
237:              echo
ocws_googlemap($ocwscc_cclon,$ocwscc_cclat,250,250)
. "\n";
238:
239:          }
240:      ?>
241:      </div><!-- end ocws_box_right -->
242:      </td>
243:      </tr>
244:      </table><!-- end of ocws_metaboxtable
-->
245:
246:  <?php
247:
248: } // end of ocwscc_mbe_function
```

This code has closed the big table, and closed the function. The Google Map function is called ocws_googlemap, and is listed later on.

The code for the second metabox is much shorter!

```
250: function ocwscc_mbe_function_sd($post) {
251: // mdeta box for short description
252: echo "<p>If you need to add a short
description for the ".CCNAME_SG.", you can add it
here. The Long Description is added above, in the
main editing box.</p>";
253:
254: $ocwscc_shortdesc= get_post_meta($post->ID,
'_ocwscc_gpshortdesc' , true ) ;
255: $ocws_wpe_settings = array(
256:      'textarea_rows' => 10,
257: );
```

```
258:  wp_editor(
htmlspecialchars_decode($ocwscc_shortdesc),
'ocwscc_gpshortdesc', $ocws_wpe_settings );
259:
260:
261: } // end ocwscc_mbe_function_sd
```

In this section, it will be noticed that the Wordpress function wp_editor produces a second editor box. The function htmlspecialchars_decode enables the html characters to be handled correctly.

Saving the Creation Cache Post

The function below is called when the Publish (or Update) button is clicked. Under these conditions, it is necessary for all the postmeta data to be updated, so there are several lines required to do this (lines 271 through 280).

```
263: function ocwscc_mbe_function_save($post_id)
{
264:   // this function will save the data used
by ocwscc_mbe_function and ocwscc_mbe_function_sd
265:
266:   // first check to ssee if the metadata has
been set
267:   if ( isset( $_POST['ocwscc_ccname'])) {
268:
269:       // now save the data
270:
271:       update_post_meta( $post_id,
'_ocwscc_ccname',  strip_tags(
$_POST['ocwscc_ccname']));
272:       update_post_meta( $post_id,
'_ocwscc_ccdate',  strip_tags(
$_POST['ocwscc_ccdate']));
273:       update_post_meta( $post_id,
'_ocwscc_cclon',  strip_tags(
$_POST['ocwscc_cclon']));
```

```
274:        update_post_meta( $post_id,
'_ocwscc_cclat', strip_tags(
$_POST['ocwscc_cclat']));
275:        update_post_meta( $post_id,
'_ocwscc_gpowner', strip_tags(
$_POST['ocwscc_gpowner']));
276:        update_post_meta( $post_id,
'_ocwscc_gpdiff', strip_tags(
$_POST['ocwscc_gpdiff']));
277:        update_post_meta( $post_id,
'_ocwscc_gpterr', strip_tags(
$_POST['ocwscc_gpterr']));
278:        update_post_meta( $post_id,
'_ocwscc_gpcountry', strip_tags(
$_POST['ocwscc_gpcountry']));
279:        update_post_meta( $post_id,
'_ocwscc_gpstate', strip_tags(
$_POST['ocwscc_gpstate']));
280:        update_post_meta( $post_id,
'_ocwscc_gpshortdesc', htmlspecialchars (
$_POST['ocwscc_gpshortdesc']));
281:

287:        ocwscc_createandsave("gpx", $post_id);
288:        ocwscc_createandsave("loc", $post_id);

291:
292:
293:   } // end if
294:
295:
296: } // end ocwscc_mbe_function_save
```

I have deleted a couple of info lines, that I included to remind me what to do next. The save function also needs to include the routines required t create or update the special downloadable .gpx and .loc files. This function is listed below.

Creating the .gpx and .loc Files

```
298: function ocwscc_createandsave($cc_fileext,
$ccpostid) {
```

```
299:    // this function checks the file extension
and directs to the appropriate builder
300:    switch ($cc_fileext) {
301:       case "gpx":
302:          $occoutput = cc_bld_gpx($ccpostid);
303:          break;
304:       case "loc":
305:          $occoutput = cc_bld_loc($ccpostid);
306:          break;
307:       default:
308:          exit(  "<p
style=\"color:#ff0000\">File extension only works
with gpx or loc</p>\n" );
309:    } // end switch
310:
311:    $ocwscc_ccname = get_post_meta( $ccpostid,
'_ocwscc_ccname', true);
312:    $cc_filename =
$ocwscc_ccname.".".$cc_fileext;
313:
314:    $cc_filepath =
OCWSCC_GPX."/".$cc_filename;
315:
    file_put_contents($cc_filepath,$occoutput);
316:
317:             $cc_zipfilename =
$ocwscc_ccname."_".$cc_fileext.".zip";
318:    $cc_zipfilepath =
OCWSCC_GPX."/".$cc_zipfilename;
319:
320:    if (file_exists($cc_zipfilepath)) {
321:    unlink($cc_zipfilepath);
322:          }
323:             $zip = new ZipArchive();
324:             $zip->open($cc_zipfilepath,
ZIPARCHIVE::CREATE);
325:
326:    $zip->addFile($cc_filepath, $cc_filename);
327:
328:    $zip->close();
329:
330:
331:
332:
333: } // end function ocwscc_createandsave
```

This function enables the files to be created and stored in the Wordpress application in their own new subfolder. That subfolder was created in the main file, and that was listed in the earlier chapter on that file, and repeated below:4

```
065: // make the new directory
066:     if (!file_exists(OCWSCC_GPX)) {
067:         mkdir(OCWSCC_GPX, 0777, true);
068:         //echo OCWSCC_GPX;
069:     }
```

The two functions required to build our xml files are not difficult. They simply involve building up a text string with the relevant code in it. This string is output to the previous function, so that it can be saved. I will quote just a little from the gpx function below. The rest can be read in the full code obtained from Github (https://github.com/pftaylor61/ocws-creationcache)

```
335: function cc_bld_gpx($ccpostid) {
336:     // builds the gpx file
337:
338:     // let's see if any metadata values exist
339:     $ocwscc_ccname = get_post_meta( $ccpostid,
'_ocwscc_ccname', true);
340:     $ocwscc_ccdate = get_post_meta( $ccpostid,
'_ocwscc_ccdate', true);
341:     $ocwscc_cclon = get_post_meta( $ccpostid,
'_ocwscc_cclon', true);
        -
355:
356:     // now let's build the file output
357:     $cc_output = "";
358:     $cc_output .= "<?xml version=\"1.0\"
encoding=\"utf-8\"?>\n";
359:     $cc_output .= "<gpx
xmlns:xsi=\"http://www.w3.org/2001/XMLSchema-
instance\"
```

```
xmlns:xsd=\"http://www.w3.org/2001/XMLSchema\"
version=\"1.0\" creator=\"Mount St Helens Creation
Center.  All  Rights  Reserved.
http://www.mshcreationcenter.org\"
xsi:schemaLocation=\"http://www.topografix.com/GPX/
1/0  http://www.topografix.com/GPX/1/0/gpx.xsd
http://www.groundspeak.com/cache/1/0
http://www.groundspeak.com/cache/1/0/cache.xsd\"
xmlns=\"http://www.topografix.com/GPX/1/0\">\n";
   360:   $cc_output .= "  <name>Creation Cache
listing from mshcreationcenter.org</name>\n";
   361:   $cc_output .= "   <desc>This  is  an
individual  cache  generated  from
mshcreationcenter.org</desc>\n";
   362:   $cc_output .= "   <author>Account
\"".$ocwscc_gpowner."\"  From
mshcreationcenter.org</author>\n";
   363:   $cc_output .= "
<email>info@mshcreationcenter.org</email>\n";
   -
   368:   $cc_output .= "   <bounds
minlat=\"".$ocwscc_cclat."\"
minlon=\"".$ocwscc_cclon."\"
maxlat=\"".$ocwscc_cclat."\"
maxlon=\"".$ocwscc_cclon."\" />\n";
   369:   $cc_output .= "   <wpt
lat=\"".$ocwscc_cclat."\"
lon=\"".$ocwscc_cclon."\">\n";
   370:   $cc_output .= "
<time>".$ocwscc_ccdate."</time>\n";
   371:   $cc_output .= "
<name>".$ocwscc_ccname."</name>\n";
   372:   $cc_output .= "
<desc>".get_the_title($ccpostid)."  by
".$ocwscc_gpowner.",  Unknown  Cache
(".$ocwscc_gpdiff."/".$ocwscc_gpterr.")</desc>\n";
   373:   $cc_output .= "
<url>".get_post_permalink($ccpostid)."</url>\n";
   374:   $cc_output .= "
<urlname>".get_the_title($ccpostid)."</urlname>\n";
   375:   $cc_output .= "   <sym>Creation Cache
Found</sym>\n";
   376:   $cc_output .= "    <type>Creation
Cache|Unknown Cache</type>\n";
   377:   $cc_output .= "   <groundspeak:cache
id=\"".$ccpostid."\"  available=\"True\"
```

```
archived=\"False\"
xmlns:groundspeak=\"http://www.groundspeak.com/cach
e/1/0\">\n";
   378:   $cc_output  .=   "
<groundspeak:name>".get_the_title($ccpostid)."</gro
undspeak:name>\n";
   379:   $cc_output  .=   "
<groundspeak:placed_by>".$ocwscc_gpowner."</grounds
peak:placed_by>\n";
     -
   393:   $cc_output  .=  "  </wpt>\n";
   394:   $cc_output  .=  "</gpx>";
   395:
   396:   return $cc_output;
   397: } // end cc_bld_gpx
```

The Google Maps Function

This function simply relies on the fact that Google Maps enables a map section of any size to be produced, using url string variables. I just built up a function that would work with four parameters - the longitude, latitude, width and height.

```
   450: function ocws_googlemap($olon,$olat,$ow,$oh)
{
   451: // this function creates a Google map from
inputted longitude and latitude
   452: $html="";
   453: $html  .=  "<iframe
src=\"https://www.google.com/maps/embed?pb=!1m14!1m
12!1m3!1d11020.919125834707!2d".$olon."!3d".$olat."
!2m3!1f0!2f0!3f0!3m2!1i1024!2i768!4f13.1!5e0!3m2!1s
en!2sus!4v1439768024304\"  width=\"".$ow."\"
height=\"".$oh."\"  frameborder=\"0\"
style=\"border:0\" allowfullscreen></iframe>";
   454: return $html;
   455: }
```

The Display

Having now got to the stage where the material for each creation cache can be created, stored and edited, and also downloaded in the .gpx or .loc files, we now need to display the information through our website. There will be two ways that the information is displayed; by a single webpage, or by an "archive" listing of all the creation caches. Generally speaking, Wordpress themes contain two templates to display this information - single.php and archive.php. The Creation Caching website uses a theme called Qohelet - more on this later. For now, let's look at the single.php template from that theme. The important section is called the_loop. Here is a typical loop.

```
        <?php while ( have_posts() ) :
the_post(); ?>

            <?php get_template_part( 'content',
get_post_format() ); ?>

            <?php
            // If comments are open or we have
at least one comment, load up the comment template
            if ( comments_open() || '0' !=
get_comments_number() ) {
                comments_template( '', true );
            }
            ?>

            <?php qohelet_content_nav( 'nav-
below' ); ?>

        <?php endwhile; // end of the loop. ?>
```

Ignoring the comments section, we see that the most important line is the get_template_part function. The archive.php template uses the same function, but with the ability to use just part of the main content, while repeating it for all posts listed on that archive page. In order to display a custom post type, it is usually easiest to create new single and archive templates. For the creation cache plugin, these are kept in a templates subfolder. Here is the code for them:

Single.php

```
<!-- HTML for the structure -->
<div id="ocwscc_mainsection">

        <?php while ( have_posts() ) : the_post();
?>

        <?php  ocwscc_get_template_part(
'content', 'single', $post ); ?>


        <?php endwhile; ?>
</div><!-- end mainsection -->
```

Archive.php

```
<!-- HTML for the structure -->
<div id="ocwscc_mainsection">
<?php
echo "<h1>Archive of ".CCNAME_PL."</h1>\n";

if(have_posts()) : while(have_posts()) :
the_post();
        ocwscc_get_template_part( 'content',
'archive', $post );
   endwhile; endif;
   ?>
</div><!-- end mainsection -->
```

Again, I have only reproduced the code for the main section. You will notice that a new function of my own creation has been called - ocwscc_get_template_part. One of the parameters enables the code to know whether a single or archive is required. The function is defined back in our functions.php file.

```
457: /* START DISPLAY FUNCTIONS */
458:
459: /* This is my own special function, to
create the main content for a Creation Cache page
*/
460: function ocwscc_get_template_part($osection,
$opagetype, $post) {
461:    // this will replace the get_template_part
function to deliver my own content
462:    if ($opagetype == 'single') { // this if
statement tests for the display of a single. The
'else' part will display an archive
463:       // initialize the function
464:       $ocwscc_ccname = get_post_meta( $post-
>ID, '_ocwscc_ccname', true);
465:       $ocwscc_ccdate = get_post_meta( $post-
>ID, '_ocwscc_ccdate', true);
466:       $ocwscc_cclon = get_post_meta( $post-
>ID, '_ocwscc_cclon', true);
467:       $ocwscc_cclat = get_post_meta( $post-
>ID, '_ocwscc_cclat', true);
468:       $ocwscc_gpname = get_post_meta( $post-
>ID, '_ocwscc_gpname', true);
469:       $ocwscc_gpowner = get_post_meta( $post-
>ID, '_ocwscc_gpowner', true);
470:       $ocwscc_gpdiff = get_post_meta( $post-
>ID, '_ocwscc_gpdiff', true);
471:       $ocwscc_gpterr = get_post_meta( $post-
>ID, '_ocwscc_gpterr', true);
472:       $ocwscc_gpcountry = get_post_meta(
$post->ID, '_ocwscc_gpcountry', true);
473:       $ocwscc_gpstate = get_post_meta( $post-
>ID, '_ocwscc_gpstate', true);
474:       $ocwscc_shortdesc=
get_post_meta($post->ID, '_ocwscc_gpshortdesc' ,
true ) ;
475:       ?>
```

```
476:                <!-- create ocwscc_infobox section
-->
477:                <div id="ocwscc_infobox">
478:                <p><strong><?php echo CCNAME_SG;
?> Details</strong></p>
479:                <table>
480:                <tr>
481:                <td
class="ocwscc_tright">Longitude:</td>
482:                <td class="ocwscc_tleft"><?php
echo $ocwscc_cclon; ?></td>
483:                </tr>
484:                <tr>
485:                <td
class="ocwscc_tright">Latitude:</td>
486:                <td class="ocwscc_tleft"><?php
echo $ocwscc_cclat; ?></td>
487:                </tr>
488:                <tr>
489:                <td
class="ocwscc_tright">Difficulty:</td>
490:                <td class="ocwscc_tleft"><?php
echo ocwscc_displaystars(5,$ocwscc_gpdiff); ?></td>
491:                </tr>
492:                <tr>
493:                <td
class="ocwscc_tright">Terrain:</td>
494:                <td class="ocwscc_tleft"><?php
echo ocwscc_displaystars(5,$ocwscc_gpterr); ?></td>
495:                </tr>
496:                <tr>
497:                <td class="ocwscc_tright">Date
Created:</td>
498:                <td class="ocwscc_tleft"><?php
echo $ocwscc_ccdate; ?></td>
499:                </tr>
500:                </table>
501:                <?php echo
ocws_googlemap($ocwscc_cclon,$ocwscc_cclat,250,2
50); ?><br /><br />
502:                <div id="ocwscc_infobox_inner"
class="ocwscc_infoboxc2">
503:                <p>To download files: right-click
on button and select &quot;Save Link As&quot;</p>
504:                <a href="<?php echo
OCWSCC_GPX_URL.$ocwscc_ccname.".gpx"; ?>"><img
```

```
     src="<?php  echo
OCWSCC_BASE_URL."/images/download_gpx.png"; ?>"
width="150" height="31" alt="Click to download .gpx
file" title=".gpx" /></a><br />
     505:            <a href="<?php  echo
OCWSCC_GPX_URL.$ocwscc_ccname.".loc"; ?>"><img
src="<?php  echo
OCWSCC_BASE_URL."/images/download_loc.png"; ?>"
width="150" height="31" alt="Click to download .loc
file" title=".loc" /></a>
     506:            </div><!--  end
ocwscc_infobox_inner -->
     507:         </div><!-- end ocwscc_infobox -->
     508:         <!-- end ocwscc_infobox section -->
     509:       <?php
     510:       $ocwscc_cacheterms = get_the_term_list(
$post_id,'cachetype');
     511:
     512:       echo  "<h1><a
href=\"".get_site_url()."/".CCSLUG."/"."\">".CCNAME
_SG."</a> #".$ocwscc_ccname."</h1>\n";
     513:              echo "<div id=\"ocwscc-
typeimg-box\" class=\"ocwscc-typeimg-box\">\n";
     514:
     515:                 echo "<img src=\"" .
ocwscc_ctype_image_url($post_id)  .  "\"
alt=\"".wp_strip_all_tags($ocwscc_cacheterms)."\"
title=\"".wp_strip_all_tags($ocwscc_cacheterms)."\"
class=\"wp-post-image ocws-typeimg-size\" />\n";
     516:               echo "</div><!-- end ocwscc-
typeimg-box -->\n";
     517:               echo "<p><strong>A cache
placed by ".$ocwscc_gpowner.".</strong> (<em>A
".$ocwscc_cacheterms." Cache.</em>)</p>\n";
     518:       echo "<p>Cache situated in
".$ocwscc_gpstate.", ".$ocwscc_gpcountry.".</p>\n";
     519:       ?>
     520:
     521:       <?php
     522:
     523:       echo "<p><strong>".CCNAME_SG."
Description</strong></p>\n";
     524:       get_template_part( $osection,
$opagetype );
     525:
```

```
526:       echo  "<p><strong>Short
Description</strong></p>\n";
527:       echo
htmlspecialchars_decode($ocwscc_shortdesc)."<br
/>";
528: ?>
529:
<p> </p><p><strong>About  <?php  echo
CCNAME_ACT; ?></strong></p>
530:                    <p><?php echo CCNAME_ACT; ?>
(<em>based on Geocaching&trade;</em>) is a real-
world, outdoor treasure hunting game using GPS-
enabled devices. Participants navigate
531:   to a specific set of GPS coordinates and
then attempt to find the geocache (container)
hidden at that location.</p>
532: <?php
533:   } // end of the 'single' display items
534:   else { // this is to display an archive
535:       if ($opagetype == 'archive') { // this
just checks that it really is an archive, and leads
to failure of any other type attenpted
536:          // initialize
537:
538:                $ocwscc_ccname  =
get_post_meta( $post->ID, '_ocwscc_ccname', true);
539:                $ocwscc_ccdate  =
get_post_meta( $post->ID, '_ocwscc_ccdate', true);
540:                $ocwscc_cclon = get_post_meta(
$post->ID, '_ocwscc_cclon', true);
541:                $ocwscc_cclat = get_post_meta(
$post->ID, '_ocwscc_cclat', true);
542:                $ocwscc_gpname  =
get_post_meta( $post->ID, '_ocwscc_gpname', true);
543:                $ocwscc_gpowner  =
get_post_meta( $post->ID, '_ocwscc_gpowner', true);
544:                $ocwscc_gpdiff  =
get_post_meta( $post->ID, '_ocwscc_gpdiff', true);
545:                $ocwscc_cachetype  =
get_the_term_list( $post->ID,'cachetype');
546:
547:                echo  the_title("<h3><a
href=\"".get_permalink()."\">","</a></h3>",fals
e)."\n";
548:                echo  "<div  id=\"ocwscc-
typeimg-box\"  class=\"ocwscc-typeimg-box\">\n";
```

```
    549:                                        echo
"<img src=\"" . ocwscc_ctype_image_url($post_id) .
"\" alt=\"".wp_strip_all_tags($ocwscc_cachetype)."\"
title=\"".wp_strip_all_tags($ocwscc_cachetype)."\"c
lass=\"wp-post-image ocws-typeimg-size-arch\"
/>\n";
    550:                                        echo
"</div><!-- end ocwscc-typeimg-box -->\n";
    551:                                        echo
"<p><strong>".CCNAME_SG."
#".$ocwscc_ccname."</strong> - A
".$ocwscc_cachetype." cache placed by
".$ocwscc_gpowner." on ".$ocwscc_ccdate."</p>\n";
    552:                   echo "<p>".the_excerpt();
    553:                   echo "<a
href=\"".get_permalink()."\">Read
more...</a></p>\n";
    554:
    555:       } // end of
archive positive test
    556:    } // end of
archive display
    557:    }  //  end
function
ocwscc_get_template_part
```

Although this is a fairly lengthy piece of code, you will recognize some important parts from it. The function is split into separate sections for the single and archive material. In both of these, the variables are loaded from the postmeta table, using the usual get_post_meta function. In

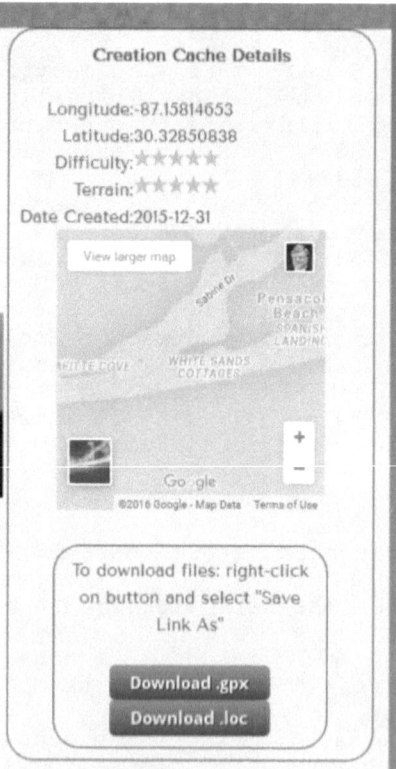

the case of the single post, this is used to build up a special box to the right of the page, containing these pieces of information. Therefore, these templates do not contain the usual sidebar, as there would be no room for it. However, the theme contains other "sidebars", which can be displayed below the main section, or in the footer, so the absence of the true sidebar does not prevent the use of widgets.

Three other issues can be noted. First is the use, once again, of the Google Maps function. Second, is the existence of a special function to display stars. And third is the code used to display a special image for the cache type.

The star function is used to display the relevant number of stars, to illustrate the difficulty and the terrain, instead of just quoting the number. The function required is as follows:

```
559: function ocwscc_displaystars($onum,$oseed) {
560:    // this will display 5 stars, indicating
quantities out of 5
561:    $ounits = intval($oseed);
562:    $odiff = $onum - $oseed;
563:    $ogray = intval($odiff);
564:    echo "<span title=\"".$oseed."\">";
565:    if ($ounits > 0) {
566:        for ($x=1; $x<=$ounits; $x++) {
567:            echo  "<img
src=\"".OCWSCC_BASE_URL."/images/goldstar.png\"
alt=\"\" title=\"".$oseed."\" />";
568:        }
569:    }
570:    if ($onum != ($ogray+$units)) {
571:        echo  "<img
src=\"".OCWSCC_BASE_URL."/images/goldgraystar.png\"
alt=\"\" title=\"".$oseed."\" />";
572:    }
```

```
573:    if ($ogray > 0) {
574:        for ($x=1; $x<=$ogray; $x++) {
575:            echo  "<img
src=\"".OCWSCC_BASE_URL."/images/graystar.png\"
alt=\"\" title=\"".$oseed."\" />";
576:        }
577:    }
578:    echo "</span>\n";
579:
580: }
```

To aid this display, the plugin images subfolder contains three star graphics - one gold, one gray, and one half gold half gray.

The category image functions will be listed in the next (short) chapter.

The final two display functions direct the Wordpress installation to find the correct templates in the plugin/templates subfolder.

```
582:   function
get_custom_post_type_template($single_template) {
583:        global $post;
584:
585:        if ($post->post_type == CCSLUG) {
586:            $single_template = OCWSCC_BASE_DIR
. '/templates/single-creationcache.php';
587:        }
588:        return $single_template;
589: }
590:
591:   function
get_custom_post_type_archtemplate($archive_templa
te) {
592:        global $post;
593:
594:        if ($post->post_type == CCSLUG) {
```

```
 595:                    $archive_template  =
OCWSCC_BASE_DIR  .  '/templates/archive-
creationcache.php';
 596:        }
 597:        return $archive_template;
 598: }
```

These functions are then called by the hooks in the main file.

```
 092:  add_filter(  'single_template',
'get_custom_post_type_template' );
 093:  add_filter(  'archive_template',
'get_custom_post_type_archtemplate' );
```

Information Page

Lines 604 though 685 give three functions, which create an information page. Normally these three functions are designed to create an admin page. I did not need an admin page, but used the same functions to create a page of information for the user of the creation cache plugin. This information is not needed for the Creation Caching website, and is simply included for other users of the plugin. I included the same information as part of the normal website information. Of course, if you wish to study the code of the three functions, you will find them in the functions.php file. The three functions are:

- ocwscc_admin_menu()
- ocwscc_info_page()
- ocws_creationcache_info_link($links)

The hooks to make use of these functions are found in the main file:

```
079: // make an info page, where the settings
normally go
080:  add_action('admin_menu',
'ocwscc_admin_menu');
081:
082: $plugin = plugin_basename(__FILE__);
083:
084: add_filter("plugin_action_links_$plugin",
'ocws_creationcache_info_link' );
```

The Edit Pages

Finally, I wanted to rearrange the columns used in the admin section, for the edit pages listings. I wanted better information in the columns, including a column which showed the special category image.

```
689: /* Functions for edit pages */
690:  function
add_new_creationcache_columns($columns) {
691:         $new_columns['cb']  =  '<input
type="checkbox" />';
692:
693:
694:         $new_columns['cachenum'] = __('Cache
#');
695:         $new_columns['title'] = _x('Creation
Cache', 'column name');
696:         $new_columns['author'] = __('Author');
697:
698:         $new_columns['cachetype'] = __('Cache
Type');
699:         $new_columns['ctype_img'] = __('Image');
700:          $new_columns['date'] = _x('Date',
'column name');
701:
702:
703:      return $new_columns;
704: }
705:
```

```
706:    function
manage_creationcache_columns($column_name,
$post_id) {
707:      // global $post;
708:              $ocwscc_cachetype =
get_the_term_list( $post_id,'cachetype');
709:    switch ($column_name) {
710:
711:    case 'cachenum':
712:        echo get_post_meta( $post_id,
'_ocwscc_ccname', true);
713:          break;
714:    case 'cachetype':
715:        echo
wp_strip_all_tags(get_the_term_list(
$post_id,'cachetype'));
716:          break;
717:          case 'ctype_img':
718:                  $ccterm_name =
wp_strip_all_tags(get_the_term_list(
$post_id,'cachetype'));
719:            $ccterm = get_term_by( 'name',
$ccterm_name,'cachetype');
720:            $ccterm_id = $ccterm->term_id;
721:                  // echo
ocws_ctype_id_image_url($ccterm_id);
722:                  echo "<img src=\"" .
ocws_ctype_id_image_url($ccterm_id) . "\"
alt=\"".wp_strip_all_tags($ocwscc_cachetype)."\"
title=\"".wp_strip_all_tags($ocwscc_cachetype)."\"
class=\"wp-post-image ocws-typeimg-size-arch\"
width=\"40\" height=\"40\" />\n";
723:                  break;
724:
725:    default:
726:        break;
727:    } // end switch
```

```
728: }
729:
730: function creationcache_sortable_columns(
$columns ) {
731:
732:    $columns['cachenum'] = 'Cache #';
733:        $columns['cachetype'] = 'Cache
Type';
734:
735:
736:    return $columns;
737: }
738:
739: /* Only run our customization on the
'edit.php' page in the admin. */
740:
741: function my_edit_creationcache_load() {
742:    add_filter( 'request',
'my_sort_creationcaches' );
743: }
744:
745: /* Sorts the creation caches. */
746: function my_sort_creationcaches( $vars ) {
747:
748:    /* Check if we're viewing the
'creationcache' post type. */
749:    if ( isset( $vars['post_type'] ) && CCSLUG
== $vars['post_type'] ) {
750:
751:        /* Check if 'orderby' is set to
'cachenum'. */
752:        /* THIS SECTION OF THE FUNCTION MAY
NEED CHECKING!! */
753:        if ( isset( $vars['orderby'] ) &&
'cachenum' == $vars['orderby'] ) {
754:
755:            /* Merge the query vars with our
custom variables. */
756:            $vars = array_merge(
757:                $vars,
758:                array(
759:                    'meta_key' => 'cachenum',
760:                    'orderby' => 'meta_value_num'
761:                )
762:            );
763:        }
```

```
764:    }
765:
766:    return $vars;
767: }
768:
769:
770: /* End Functions for edit pages */
```

690 - 704 shows the new column definitions, to replace the standard columns. 706 - 728 populates these columns. The most sophisticated column population is that of the image column, defined in lines 720-723.

The function creationcache_sortable_columns allows the columns to be sorted by other headings. The rest of the code just defines how that sorting can take place.

And that brings us to the end of the large functions.php file. Now we need to look at how the category images were put in place.

Category Images

There is a very useful Wordpress plugin, from zahlen.net, called Category Images. In the spirit of reusing open source material, I have cannibalised that code, to add to the Creation Cache plugin.

```
013:
add_action('cachetype_add_form_fields',
'ocwscc_add_taxonomy_field');
    014:
    add_action('cachetype_edit_form_fields',
'ocwscc_edit_taxonomy_field');
    015:        add_filter( 'manage_edit-
cachetype_columns', 'ocwscc_taxonomy_columns' );
    016:        add_filter(
'manage_cachetype_custom_column',
'ocwscc_taxonomy_column', 10, 3 );
    017:
    018: function ocwscc_add_style() {
    019:    echo '<style type="text/css"
media="screen">
    020:        th.column-thumb {width:60px;}
    021:        .form-field img.taxonomy-image
{border:1px solid #eee;max-width:300px;max-
height:300px;}
    022:        .inline-edit-row fieldset .thumb label
span.title {width:48px;height:48px;border:1px solid
#eee;display:inline-block;}
    023:        .column-thumb span
{width:48px;height:48px;border:1px solid
#eee;display:inline-block;}
    024:        .inline-edit-row fieldset .thumb
img,.column-thumb img {width:48px;height:48px;}
    025:    </style>';
    026: }
```

Lines 13-16 contain the hooks and filters required, to use the category images. These images will only apply to the

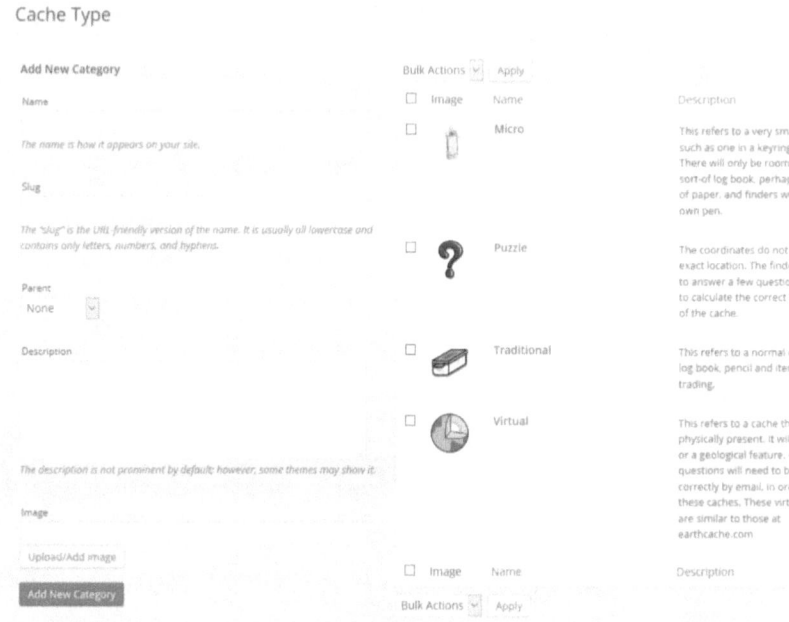

taxonomy for the Creation Caches, which I call Cache type, whereas the original zahlen plugin worked for any post type.

The ocwscc_add_style function produces some css, which allows the images to be displayed very small.

Next we have the functions, mentioned in the hooks above, to add and edit the cache Type images.

```
028: // add image field in add form
029: function ocwscc_add_taxonomy_field() {
030:    if (get_bloginfo('version') >= 3.5)
031:       wp_enqueue_media();
032:    else {
033:       wp_enqueue_style('thickbox');
```

```
034:       wp_enqueue_script('thickbox');
035:     }
036:
037:   echo '<div class="form-field">
038:       <label for="creationcache_image">' .
__('Image', 'creationcache') . '</label>
039:       <input  type="text"
name="creationcache_image" id="creationcache_image"
value="" />
040:       <br/>
041:       <button
class="ocwscc_upload_image_button
button">Upload/Add image</button>
042:   </div>'.ocwscc_upload_script();
043: }
044:
045: // add image field in edit form
046: function ocwscc_edit_taxonomy_field() {
047:   if (get_bloginfo('version') >= 3.5)
048:       wp_enqueue_media();
049:   else {
050:       wp_enqueue_style('thickbox');
051:       wp_enqueue_script('thickbox');
052:   }
053:
054:           $term_id = "";
055:
056:           if (isset($_GET['tag_ID'])){
057:           $term_id = trim($_GET['tag_ID']);
058:
059:           }
060:   /* if (ocwscc_creationcache_image_url(
$term_id, NULL, TRUE ) == OCWSCC_IMAGE_PLACEHOLDER)
061:       $image_url = "";
062:   else */
063:       $image_url =
ocws_ctype_id_image_url($term_id);
064:               $image_url2 = "";
065:               if (!($image_url ==
OCWSCC_IMAGE_PLACEHOLDER)){
066:                   $image_url2 =
$image_url;
067:                   }
068:               // $image_url =
ocwscc_creationcache_image_url( $term_id, NULL,
TRUE );
```

```
069:    echo '<tr class="form-field">
070:        <th scope="row" valign="top"><label
for="creationcache_image">Image</label></th>
071:        <td><img class="taxonomy-image" src="' .
$image_url  . '"/><br/><input type="text"
name="creationcache_image" id="creationcache_image"
value="'.$image_url2.'" /><br />
072:        <button
class="ocwscc_upload_image_button
button">Upload/Add image</button>
073:        <button
class="ocwscc_remove_image_button button">Remove
image</button>
074:        </td>
075:    </tr>'.ocwscc_upload_script();
076: }
```

Since I am creating the ability for a Cache Type image, it makes sense for there to be a default image, in case the user has not defined one. This default image is placed in the images subfolder, and is referenced here.

After this, the zahlen plugin added an unusual function, whereby some Javascript was created on the fly. This Javascript enables the upload button to choose an image an upload it to the application. I find this PHP-generated Javascript to be rather odd, and I debated trying to work out how to place the script in a separate Javascript file. However, at the moment it just works, so I am a bit loath to tidy it up, much as I would like to.

```
078: // upload using wordpress upload
079: function ocwscc_upload_script() {
080:    return '<script type="text/javascript">
081:        jQuery(document).ready(function($) {
082:            var wordpress_ver =
"'.get_bloginfo("version").'", upload_button;
```

```
083:

$(".ocwscc_upload_image_button").click(function(eve
nt) {
    084:             upload_button = $(this);
    085:             var frame;
    086:             if (wordpress_ver >= "3.5") {
    087:                 event.preventDefault();
    088:                 if (frame) {
    089:                     frame.open();
    090:                     return;
    091:                 }
    092:                 frame = wp.media();
    093:                 frame.on( "select", function()
{
    094:                     // Grab the selected
attachment.
    095:                     var attachment =
frame.state().get("selection").first();
    096:                     frame.close();
    097:                     if
(upload_button.parent().prev().children().hasClass
("tax_list")) {
    098:
upload_button.parent().prev().children().val(attach
ment.attributes.url);
    099:
upload_button.parent().prev().prev().children().att
r("src", attachment.attributes.url);
    100:                     }
    101:                     else
    102:
$("#creationcache_image").val(attachment.attribute
s.url);
    103:                 });
    104:                 frame.open();
    105:             }
    106:             else {
    107:                 tb_show("", "media-
upload.php?type=image&amp;TB_iframe=true");
    108:                 return false;
    109:             }
    110:         });
```

```
    111:
    112:

$(".ocwscc_remove_image_button").click(function() {
    113:              $(".taxonomy-image").attr("src",
"'.OCWSCC_IMAGE_PLACEHOLDER.'");
    114:
    $("#creationcache_image").val("");
    115:

$(this).parent().siblings(".title").children("img"
).attr("src","' . OCWSCC_IMAGE_PLACEHOLDER . '");
    116:              $(".inline-edit-col
:input[name=\'creationcache_image\']").val("");
    117:            return false;
    118:         });
    119:
    120:          if (wordpress_ver < "3.5") {
    121:              window.send_to_editor   =
function(html) {
    122:               imgurl   =
$("img",html).attr("src");
    123:               if
(upload_button.parent().prev().children().hasClass
("tax_list")) {
    124:

upload_button.parent().prev().children().val(imgu
rl);
    125:

upload_button.parent().prev().prev().children().att
r("src", imgurl);
    126:            }
    127:            else
    128:
    $("#creationcache_image").val(imgurl);
    129:             tb_remove();
    130:          }
    131:       }
    132:
    133:          $(".editinline").click(function() {
    134:              var  tax_id   =
$(this).parents("tr").attr("id").substr(4);
    135:              var thumb = $("#tag-"+tax_id+"
.thumb img").attr("src");
```

```
136:
137:                    if   (thumb  !=   "'   .
OCWSCC_IMAGE_PLACEHOLDER  .  '") {
138:                    $(".inline-edit-col
:input[name=\'creationcache_image\']").val(thumb);
139:                    } else {
140:                    $(".inline-edit-col
:input[name=\'creationcache_image\']").val("");
141:                    }
142:
143:                    $(".inline-edit-col  .title
img").attr("src",thumb);
144:              });
145:          });
146:    </script>';
147: }
```

These next two functions manipulate the addresses of the images, so that their urls can be stored in the database, and retrieved from it.

```
149: // save our taxonomy image while edit or
save term
150:
add_action('edit_term','ocwscc_save_taxonomy_ima
ge');
151:
add_action('create_term','ocwscc_save_taxonomy_ima
ge');
152:  function
ocwscc_save_taxonomy_image($term_id) {
153:      if(isset($_POST['creationcache_image']))
154:
update_option('ocwscc_creationcache_image'.$term_id,
$_POST['creationcache_image'], NULL);
155: }
156:
157: // get attachment ID by image url
158:  function
ocwscc_get_attachment_id_by_url($image_src) {
159:      global $wpdb;
160:      $query = $wpdb->prepare("SELECT ID FROM
$wpdb->posts WHERE guid = %s", $image_src);
161:      $id = $wpdb->get_var($query);
```

```
162:        return (!empty($id)) ? $id : NULL;
163: }
```

This is followed by a function that takes care of displaying the default image in the right place.

```
165: // get taxonomy image url for the given
term_id (Place holder image by default)
166:    function
ocwscc_creationcache_image_url($term_id = NULL,
$size = 'full', $return_placeholder = FALSE) {
-
177:
178:            $creationcache_image_url =
get_option('ocwscc_creationcache_image'.$term_id);
179:        if(!empty($creationcache_image_url)) {
180:            $attachment_id =
ocwscc_get_attachment_id_by_url($creationcache_imag
e_url);
181:        if(!empty($attachment_id)) {
182:            $creationcache_image_url =
wp_get_attachment_image_src($attachment_id, $size);
183:            $creationcache_image_url =
$creationcache_image_url[0];
184:        }
185:    }
186:
187:    if ($return_placeholder)
188:        return ($creationcache_image_url != '')
? $creationcache_image_url :
OCWSCC_IMAGE_PLACEHOLDER;
189:    else
190:        return $creationcache_image_url;
191: }
```

The edit list for any type of posts usually contains a quick edit capability. I wanted the Creation cache image to be editable in the quick edit, as well as the full edit box.

```
193:    function
ocwscc_quick_edit_custom_box($column_name, $screen,
$name) {
```

```
194:    if ($column_name == 'thumb')
195:        echo '<fieldset>
196:        <div class="thumb inline-edit-col">
197:            <label>
198:                <span class="title"><img src=""
alt="Thumbnail"/></span>
199:                <span  class="input-text-
wrap"><input type="text" name="creationcache_image"
value="" class="tax_list" /></span>
200:                <span class="input-text-wrap">
201:                    <button
class="ocwscc_upload_image_button
button">Upload/Add image</button>
202:                    <button
class="ocwscc_remove_image_button button">Remove
image</button>
203:                </span>
204:            </label>
205:        </div>
206:    </fieldset>';
207: }
```

The next two functions are referred to in the filters at the top of the file. These enable the columns to be manipulated and populated with the images.

```
216: function ocwscc_taxonomy_columns( $columns )
{
217:    $new_columns = array();
218:    $new_columns['cb'] = $columns['cb'];
219:    $new_columns['thumb'] = 'Image';
220:
221:    unset( $columns['cb'] );
222:
223:    return array_merge( $new_columns, $columns
);
224: }
225:
    _
235: function ocwscc_taxonomy_column( $columns,
$column, $id ) {
236:    if ( $column == 'thumb' )
237:        $columns  =  '<span><img  src="'  .
ocwscc_creationcache_image_url($id, 'thumbnail',
```

```
TRUE) . '" alt="Thumbnail" class="wp-post-image"
/></span>';
  238:
  239:   return $columns;
  240: }
```

One tiny function enables the text in the upload button to be changed, depending on circumstances. Also, the hooks are added to call the relevant functions above.

```
  242: // Change 'insert into post' to 'use this
image'
  243:   function
ocwscc_change_insert_button_text($safe_text, $text)
{
  244:       return str_replace("Insert into Post",
"Use this image", $text);
  245: }
  246:
  247: // Style the image in category list
  248: if ( strpos( $_SERVER['SCRIPT_NAME'], 'edit-
tags.php' ) > 0 ) {
  249:   add_action( 'admin_head',
'ocwscc_add_style' );
  250:   add_action('quick_edit_custom_box',
'ocwscc_quick_edit_custom_box', 10, 3);
  251:   add_filter("attribute_escape",
"ocwscc_change_insert_button_text", 10, 2);
  252: }
```

Then I needed a function that would associate the correct Cache Type image with each Creation Cache.

```
  254: // display taxonomy image for the given
term_id
  255: function ocwscc_creationcache_image($term_id
= NULL, $size = 'full', $attr = NULL, $echo = TRUE)
{
  256:   if (!$term_id) {
  257:       if (is_category())
  258:           $term_id = get_query_var('cat');
  259:       elseif (is_tax()) {
```

```
260:          $current_term = get_term_by('slug',
get_query_var('term'), get_query_var('taxonomy'));
261:          $term_id = $current_term->term_id;
262:     }
263:   }
264:
265:          $taxonomy_image_url =
get_option('ocwscc_creationcache_image'.$term_id);
266:     if(!empty($taxonomy_image_url)) {
267:          $attachment_id =
ocwscc_get_attachment_id_by_url($taxonomy_image_u
rl);
268:        if(!empty($attachment_id))
269:          $taxonomy_image =
wp_get_attachment_image($attachment_id, $size,
FALSE, $attr);
270:     else {
271:        $image_attr = '';
272:        if(is_array($attr)) {
273:          if(!empty($attr['class']))
274:             $image_attr .= '
class="'.$attr['class'].'" ';
275:          if(!empty($attr['alt']))
276:             $image_attr .= '
alt="'.$attr['alt'].'" ';
277:          if(!empty($attr['width']))
278:             $image_attr .= '
width="'.$attr['width'].'" ';
279:          if(!empty($attr['height']))
280:             $image_attr .= '
height="'.$attr['height'].'" ';
281:          if(!empty($attr['title']))
282:             $image_attr .= '
title="'.$attr['title'].'" ';
283:        }
284:        $taxonomy_image = '<img
src="'.$taxonomy_image_url.'" '.$image_attr.'/>';
285:     }
286:   }
287:
288:   if ($echo)
289:      echo $taxonomy_image;
290:   else
291:      return $taxonomy_image;
292: }
```

The final two functions automatically select the correct image for a cache's id, or for a cache type id.

```
294: /*
295:  * This function finds the appropriate cache
image url from the creation cache id
296:  */
297: function ocwscc_ctype_image_url($cache_id){
298:               $cimage_url   =
OCWSCC_IMAGE_PLACEHOLDER;
299:          $cimage_url_id = "";
300:          if (!$cache_id){
301:               $terms = get_the_terms(
$cache_id , 'cachetype' );
302:               if($terms) {
303:                    foreach( $terms as
$term ) {
304:
$cimage_url_id = $term->term_id;
305:                    }
306:               }
307:               $cimage_url_str =
"ocwscc_creationcache_image".strval($cimage_url_id);
308:                              if
(!get_option($cimage_url_str)){
309:                    $cimage_url =
OCWSCC_IMAGE_PLACEHOLDER;
310:               } else {
311:                    $cimage_url =
get_option($cimage_url_str);
312:               }
313:          }
314:
315:          return $cimage_url;
316: }
317:
318: /*
319:  * This function finds the appropriate cache
image url from the cachetype id
320:  */
321: function ocws_ctype_id_image_url($ctype_id){
322:          $cimage_url_str   =
"ocwscc_creationcache_image".strval($ctype_id);
323:                              if
(!get_option($cimage_url_str)){
```

```
324:                        $cimage_url =
OCWSCC_IMAGE_PLACEHOLDER;
325:               } else {
326:                        $cimage_url =
get_option($cimage_url_str);
327:               }
328:      return $cimage_url;
329: }
```

As I said above, none of this code is original to me. It is all a tweaking and simplification from the code found at zahlen.net. This is general, however, in any open source system. The beauty is in being able to reuse other peoples' code, just as you can now reuse mine.

That brings us to the end of the files required for the Creation Cache plugin. However, the Creation caching website required far more than just the Creation Cache plugin. I also produced a main theme and a child theme for the site, as well as drawing up a plugin to display images in a Javascript slider. I think we will deal next with the slider.

A Slider plugin

There are a lot of plugins out there, that will produce sliders. However, it is nice to have a neat one of my own. Of course, this is not really my own. The information required to build the plugin came from a tutorial by Ciprian Turcu, published at http://code.tutsplus.com/tutorials/build-a-slideshow-plugin-for-wordpress--wp-25789. I just adapted this very slightly for my own purposes. Mr Turco did not invent the code himself either. Dev7Studios have produced a premium slider, using some Jquery code that they have written called Nivo. However, the actual Nivo scripts were released by Dev7Studios into the Open Source, so that other people could use the scripts to develop their own sliders. That is the code that Ciprian Turco used in his tutorial.

As with the Creation Cache plugin, a new folder is needed inside the plugins folder, and a file with the same name created as the main file. The first few lines of this file gives the essential information for the plugin to work with. This information is similar to that used for the Creation cache plugin.

File ocws-slider.php

```
001: <?php
002: /*
003:     Plugin Name: OCWS Slider Plugin
004:     Description: This is a full featured
slider plugin. It is actually a simple
implementation of a nivo slideshow into WordPress.
It utilizes the nivo slider jQuery code, following
```

a tutorial by Ciprian Turcu. A couple of OCWS custom features have been added. Make sure you include the shortcode [ocwssl-shortcode] in any page where you wish the slider to appear.
```
005:      Author: Paul Taylor
006:      Version: 0.3
007:         Plugin URI:
http://oldcastleweb.com/pws/plugins
008:         Author URI:
http://oldcastleweb.com/pws/about
009:      License: GPL2
010:         GitHub Plugin URI:
https://github.com/pftaylor61/ocws-slider
011:      GitHub Branch:    master
012: */
```

Custom Post Type

The next two sections, reproduced below, give the definitions, and also define the slider custom post type. This post type is easier, because the slider "posts" won't be displayed as separate pages, but only so that the slider can have elements to work through.

```
014: /* Essential Initialization Definitions */
015: define('SLSLUG', 'ocwsslider');
016: define('SLNAME_SG', 'Slider Image');
017: define('SLNAME_PL', 'Slider Images');
018: define("OCWSSL_BASE_DIR",dirname(__FILE__));
019: define("OCWSSL_BASE_URL",plugins_url( '',
__FILE__ ));
020:
define("OCWSSL_IMAGES_URL",OCWSSL_BASE_URL."/imag
es");
021:
022:
023:
024: function ocwssl_init() {
025:      add_shortcode('ocwssl-shortcode',
'ocwssl_function');
026:      $args = array(
027:         'public' => true,
```

```
028:          'labels' => array(
029:             'name' => __( 'Slider Images' ,
SLSLUG),
030:             'singular_name' => __(
SLNAME_SG , SLSLUG),
031:             'add_new' => __( 'Add New',
SLSLUG ),
032:             'add_new_item' => __( 'Add New
'.SLNAME_SG, SLSLUG ),
033:             'edit_item' => __( 'Edit
'.SLNAME_SG, SLSLUG ),
034:             'new_item' => __( 'New
'.SLNAME_SG, SLSLUG ),
035:             'view_item' => __( 'View
'.SLNAME_SG, SLSLUG ),
036:             'search_items' => __( 'Search
'.SLNAME_PL, SLSLUG ),
037:             'not_found' => __( 'No
'.SLNAME_PL.' found', SLSLUG ),
038:             'not_found_in_trash' => __(
'No '.SLNAME_PL.' found in Trash', SLSLUG ),
039:             'parent_item_colon' => __(
'Parent '.SLNAME_SG.':', SLSLUG ),
040:             'menu_name' => __( SLNAME_PL,
SLSLUG ),
041:                        ),
042:             'menu_icon'    =>
OCWSSL_IMAGES_URL.'/palmtree16x16.png',
043:          'show_ui' => true,
044:          'supports' => array(
045:             'title',
046:             'thumbnail',
047:
048:          )
049:       );
050:       register_post_type('ocwssl_images',
$args);
051:
add_action('add_meta_boxes','ocwssl_mbe_create');
052:
053:       add_image_size('ocwssl_widget', 150, 83,
true);
054:       add_image_size('ocwssl_function', 600,
280, true);
055:       add_image_size('ocwssl_thin',600, 40,
true);
```

```
056: }
057: add_theme_support( 'post-thumbnails' );
058: add_action('init', 'ocwssl_init');
```

Lines 57-58 are the hooks needed, to allow themes to support the slider.

Pre-Written Scripts

Really, the only bit of proprietary code that I added was line 55. The tutorial gave two image sizes for sliders - one for a large slider, and one for display inside a widget. However, I thought it would be good for the Creation Caching site to have a long thin slider. I did not need the other two sizes, but decided to leave them in, and follow the tutorial in entirety, so that I had a fully working plugin that I could use again in other projects.

The Nivo scripts were downloaded from Dev7Studios, and placed in a subfolder called nivo-slider. These scripts were not edited in any way. If you download the plugin from Github (address shown in the first code snippet in this chapter), then you can investigate them, and alter them all you like. But I have used them unaltered. In order to access them, I needed to add a very simple Javascript file of my own.

```
01: /*
02:  * To change this license header, choose
License Headers in Project Properties.
03:  * To change this template file, choose Tools
| Templates
04:  * and open the template in the editor.
05:  */
06:
```

```
07: jQuery(document).ready(function($) {
08:     $('#slider').nivoSlider();
09: });
```

To get all the files to work, all I then needed to do was to enqueue this file, and the main nivo slider file.

```
077: function ocwssl_register_scripts() {
078:     if (!is_admin()) {
079:         // register
080:         wp_register_script('ocwssl_nivo-
script', plugins_url('nivo-
slider/jquery.nivo.slider.js', __FILE__), array(
'jquery' ));
081:         wp_register_script('ocwssl_script',
plugins_url('script.js', __FILE__));
082:
083:         // enqueue
084:         wp_enqueue_script('ocwssl_nivo-
script');
085:         wp_enqueue_script('ocwssl_script');
086:     }
087: }
088:
089: function ocwssl_register_styles() {
090:     // register
091:      wp_register_style('ocwssl_styles',
plugins_url('nivo-slider/nivo-slider.css',
__FILE__));
092:     wp_register_style('ocwssl_styles_theme',
plugins_url('nivo-
slider/themes/default/default.css', __FILE__));
093:
094:     // enqueue
095:     wp_enqueue_style('ocwssl_styles');
096:     wp_enqueue_style('ocwssl_styles_theme');
097: }
```

The enqueued stylesheets shown were also part of the nivo slider package, unaltered by me.

As I pointed out before, no display of the Slider custom post type was needed. Instead, a function was built which would simply page through the_loop of all the slides, so that they could be displayed.

```
099: /* querying the loop to get the slides */
100:  function
ocwssl_function($type='ocwssl_function') {
101:      $args = array(
102:          'post_type' => 'ocwssl_images',
103:          'posts_per_page' => 5
104:      );
105:      $result = '<div class="slider-wrapper
theme-default">';
106:          $result .=  '<div  id="slider"
class="nivoSlider">';
107:
108:      //the loop
109:      $loop = new WP_Query($args);
110:      while ($loop->have_posts()) {
111:          $loop->the_post();
112:
113:              $the_url =
wp_get_attachment_image_src(get_post_thumbnail_id($
post->ID), $type);
114:              $result .='<img
title="'.get_the_title().'" src="' . $the_url[0] .
'" data-thumb="' . $the_url[0] . '" alt=""/>';
115:      }
116:      $result .= '</div>';
117:      $result .='<div id = "htmlcaption" class
= "nivo-html-caption">';
118:      $result .='<strong>This</strong> is an
example of a <em>HTML</em> caption with <a href =
"#">a link</a>.';
119:      $result .='</div>';
120:      $result .='</div>';
121:      return $result;
122: }
```

The theme that I am using has a banner section in its header. So I was able to open the header.php file, and add this code into that banner:

```
<?php if ( is_front_page() ) {
                                echo
ocwssl_function('ocwssl_thin');
      } ?>
```

Although this method works, I have now made a system that will only work for this site. If I try to use this theme without the slider plugin, or the plugin without the theme, I will get a problem. A more general way to use the plugin is to use the shortcode mentioned below, added straight into a page. But, for my purposes, the above system works better. Notice that the function uses the slider size as a parameter. Notice also the "if" test, so that the slider only appears on the home page, and not on any other page.

Widget

For my purposes, the code is now over. I simply need to add this function to the header of the main page of my theme. I will show you how I did this earlier. However, the main plugin allows for two other methods of displaying the slider. The first is by shortcode, and has already been quoted at line 25. It allows for the following shortcode to be added to a post.

```
[ocwssl-shortcode]
```

The other is to display the slider in a widget. The rest of the code quoted simply creates the widget, and allows the slider to be displayed through it.

```
124: /* material for slideshow widget */
125: function ocwssl_widgets_init() {
126:     register_widget('ocwssl_Widget');
127: }
128:
129: add_action('widgets_init',
'ocwssl_widgets_init');
130:
131: class ocwssl_Widget extends WP_Widget {
132:
133:     public function __construct() {
134:         parent::__construct('ocwssl_Widget',
'OCWS Slideshow', array('description' => __('A Nivo
Slideshow Widget, from OCWS', 'text_domain')));
135:     } // end public function __construct
136:
137:     public function form($instance) {
138:     if (isset($instance['title'])) {
139:         $title = $instance['title'];
140:     }
141:     else {
142:         $title = __('Widget Slideshow',
'text_domain');
143:     }
144:     ?>
145:         <p>
146:             <label for="<?php echo $this-
>get_field_id('title'); ?>"><?php _e('Title:');
?></label>
147:             <input class="widefat" id="<?php
echo $this->get_field_id('title'); ?>" name="<?php
echo $this->get_field_name('title'); ?>" type="text"
value="<?php echo esc_attr($title); ?>" />
148:         </p>
149:     <?php
150:     } // end public function form
151:
152:     public function update($new_instance,
$old_instance) {
153:         $instance = array();
```

```
154:          $instance['title']  =
strip_tags($new_instance['title']);
155:
156:      return $instance;
157:      } // end public function update
158:
159:      public function widget($args, $instance)
{
160:      extract($args);
161:      // the title
162:      $title = apply_filters('widget_title',
$instance['title']);
163:      echo $before_widget;
164:      if (!empty($title))
165:          echo $before_title . $title .
$after_title;
166:      echo ocwssl_function('ocwssl_widget');
167:      echo $after_widget;
168:      } // end public function widget
169:
170: } // end class ocwssl_Widget
```

The result of using this free tutorial, and the open source nivo slider scripts, is that I gained a very useful new free plugin, that I will be able to use over and again.

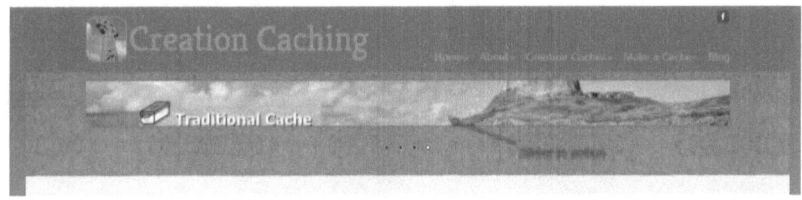

Qohelet Theme

My usual method, up to the design of the Creation Caching website, has been to select a suitable theme, and then to tweak it, by using a child theme. But, with this site, I decided it was high time I had a theme of my own.

This is not as daunting a task as might at first appear, because a number of very helpful people have built so-called starter themes, from which we can design our own themes. Once again, we are building on other people's open source foundations. So, although a theme is a complex set of programming, containing a lot of files, most of these have been put together for me in starter themes.

My criteria was that I needed my own starter theme, on which I could build. In particular, I wanted to be able to make easy-to-use child themes, based on my own foundational theme.

I called my foundational theme Qohelet. This is from the Hebrew word for Teacher or Preacher, and is the *nom de plume* used by the writer of the biblical book Ecclesiastes - probably King Solomon. The child theme that I designed for this site is called Golden Bowl, which is a term used in Ecclesiastes 12, probably representing the brain.

Underscores

Hardly anyone starts from scratch anymore. Why should we? We are all building on Wordpress. The whole Wordpress application is produced by a company called Automattic. The same company recently decided to make the ultimate blank starter theme for people to build on, so they produced a theme which they called _s. Yes, it's name is _s. We have to be able to pronounce this name, so we call it Underscores.

The Underscores theme is available from underscores.me. The raw theme contains a full set of templates, together with a full set of stylesheets. However, most of the styles are blank, or very basic. The idea is that the designer can go through these styles, a bit at a time, amending and altering until he has a complete theme. Underscores has been designed to be responsive, in a general sort of way. A responsive theme is one that alters itsekf on the fly, depending on the size of the display media, so that it looks good on any device, whether PC screen, tablet or smartphone.

My first thought was to learn how to adapt Underscores. The web contains lots of tutorials, to enable people to do this. One of the best is at the education site lynda.com, where one designer goes through, bit by bit, snippet by snippet, how he made a theme called Simone from Underscores. I strongly recommend that tutorial, if you intend to start designing themes, even if, like me, you take a shortcut, and even though the lynda.com site is not free, but requires a paid subscription. You should also download the finished Simone theme, so that you can see its relationship to Underscores. However, I soon discovered that there were people who had built more advanced themes, on top of Underscores, yet still released them as open source starter themes. My favorite of these was:

Quark

The Quark theme can be found at: quarktheme.com

Once you have downloaded it, you will discover the following.

- The theme is entirely built upon Underscores, and has itself been deliberately released as a starter theme.
- The author, Antony Horton, has painstakingly altered the CSS of Underscores to conform with CSS3. In so doing, he has added a fully responsive 12 column grid system, which is the latest idea in responsive design, because the 2 columns can easily slide past each other in different environments and media sizes.
- Several other useful open source technologies have been added, such as Modernizr, which is a Javascript system, which automatically detects the users' browser capabilities, and adjust the display accordingly. Programming this

feature alone would have taken weeks. Modernizr is from https://modernizr.com/

- Horton has added a specially written stylesheet called Normalize, which makes sure that each browser renders elements correctly. Normalize is found at https://github.com/necolas/normalize.css
- The Options Framework was added, so that the theme has a ready-made admin panel, which can easily be adapted by the user. Options Framework is from http://wptheming.com/options-framework-theme/
- Much of the html code that Quark uses comes from the HTML 5 Boilerplate. http://html5boilerplate.com/
- Just for fun, Horton has added support for the extremely useful and beautiful custom font elements in Font Awesome - http://fortawesome.github.io/Font-Awesome/

So, Quark has added to Underscores, by using lots of other open source technologies, and bringing them together in a user friendly way. My job was to take this theme, and tweak it for my own purposes.

My Additions to Qohelet

All of these technologies can be readily accessed and downloaded by the reader. My own Qohelet theme can be found at: https://github.com/pftaylor61/qohelet.

The main file in a theme, unlike a plugin, is a css file. In fact, it is always called style.css. Here are the first few lines of Qohelet's style.css

File style.css

```
0001: /*
0002: Theme Name: Qohelet
0003: Theme URI:
http://www.oldcastleweb.com/pws/themes/qohelet/
0004: Author: Paul Taylor
0005: Author URI: http://www.oldcastleweb.com
0006: Description: Qohelet is a fully responsive
theme for Wordpress. It has been built on the
shoulders of giants, utilizing a number of other
technologies, such as: 1. The Quark starter theme
by Anthony Horton. 2. Quark is in turn built upon
Underscores by Automattix. 3. Quark utilizes
Normalize, Modernizr and Options Framework. 4. Many
other smaller amounts of other technologies have
been incorporated, so that I did not re-invent the
wheel.
0007: Version: 0.4
0008: License: GNU General Public License v2 or
later
0009: License URI:
http://www.gnu.org/licenses/gpl-2.0.html
0010: Tags: black, gray, dark, light, one-column,
two-columns, right-sidebar, fluid-layout,
responsive-layout, custom-background, custom-header,
custom-menu, editor-style, featured-image-header,
featured-images, full-width-template, microformats,
post-formats, sticky-post, theme-options, threaded-
comments, translation-ready
0011: Text Domain: qohelet
0012: GitHub Theme URI:
https://github.com/pftaylor61/qohelet
0013: GitHub Branch:    master
0014: */
```

With over 2400 lines, it would add nothing to the sum of human knowledge for me to reproduce this entire file in this book, especially as most of the code is simply used unaltered from Underscores and/or Quark. However, those who have gone before me have released their code in such a way that I can register my theme as a full theme. I am very pleased to be standing on the shoulders of giants, to be able to produce this theme.

My initial tweaks involved changing the fonts. Quark had been produced, using some Google fonts. It was not difficult for me to alter these fonts. I decided that my main headings would be in a serif font, called Kreon, while the main text would use Tenor Sans. Neither of these fonts are common fonts on users' computers, but can be added, using Google fonts.

The following two functions are found in the functions.php file, and produce the urls required for the fonts.

```
0142: /**
0143:  * Returns the Google font stylesheet URL,
if available.
0144:  *
0145:  * The use of Tenor Sans and Kreon by
default is localized. For languages that use
characters not supported by the fonts, the fonts
can be disabled.
0146:  *
0147:  * @since Qohelet 0.0.1
0148:  *
0149:  * @return string Font stylesheet or empty
string if disabled.
0150:  */
0151: function qohelet_fonts_url() {
0152: $fonts_url = '';
0153: $subsets = 'latin';
0154:
0155: /* translators: If there are characters in
your language that are not supported by Tenor Sans,
translate this to 'off'.
0156:  * Do not translate into your own language.
```

```
0157:    */
0158: $tenor_sans = _x( 'on', 'Tenor Sans font:
on or off', 'qohelet' );
0159:
0160: /* translators: To add an additional Tenor
Sans character subset specific to your language,
translate this to 'greek', 'cyrillic' or
'vietnamese'.
0161:    * Do not translate into your own language.
0162:    */
0163: $subset = _x( 'no-subset', 'Tenor Sans
font: add new subset (cyrillic)', 'qohelet' );
0164:
0165: if ( 'cyrillic' == $subset )
0166:    $subsets .= ',cyrillic';
0167:
0168: /* translators: If there are characters in
your language that are not supported by Kreon,
translate this to 'off'.
0169:    * Do not translate into your own language.
0170:    */
0171: $kreon = _x( 'on', 'Kreon font: on or off',
'qohelet' );
0172:
0173: if ( 'off' !== $tenor_sans || 'off' !==
$kreon ) {
0174:    $font_families = array();
0175:
0176:    if ( 'off' !== $pt_sans )
0177:       $font_families[] =
'Tenor+Sans:400,400italic,700,700italic';
0178:
0179:    if ( 'off' !== $Kreon )
0180:       $font_families[] = 'Kreon:400';
0181:
0182:    $protocol = is_ssl() ? 'https' :
'http';
0183:    $query_args = array(
0184:       'family' => implode( '|',
$font_families ),
0185:       'subset' => $subsets,
0186:    );
0187:    $fonts_url = add_query_arg( $query_args,
"$protocol://fonts.googleapis.com/css" );
0188: }
0189:
```

```
0190:    return $fonts_url;
0191:  }
0192:
0193:
0194:  /**
0195:   * Adds additional stylesheets to the
TinyMCE editor if needed.
0196:   *
0197:   * @since Qohelet 0.0.1
0198:   *
0199:   * @param string $mce_css CSS path to load
in TinyMCE.
0200:   * @return string The filtered CSS paths
list.
0201:   */
0202:  function qohelet_mce_css( $mce_css ) {
0203:    $fonts_url = qohelet_fonts_url();
0204:
0205:    if ( empty( $fonts_url ) ) {
0206:        return $mce_css;
0207:    }
0208:
0209:    if ( !empty( $mce_css ) ) {
0210:        $mce_css .= ',';
0211:    }
0212:
0213:    $mce_css .= esc_url_raw( str_replace( ',',
'%2C', $fonts_url ) );
0214:
0215:    return $mce_css;
0216:  }
0217:  add_filter( 'mce_css', 'qohelet_mce_css' );
```

These fonts are enqueued elsewhere in functions.php, thus:

```
0407:  $fonts_url = qohelet_fonts_url();
0408:  if ( !empty( $fonts_url ) ) {
0409:      wp_enqueue_style( 'qohelet-fonts',
esc_url_raw( $fonts_url ), array(), null );
0410:  }
```

Then there were some minor style tweaks, chaging the default text in the footer, and the default background color, and the image for the banner area. These were minor and very easy.

Backup Options

The one major area that I wanted to add was a system to backup the options, once made. I get fed up of transferring sites from PC to remote server and back again, and finding that I have to carefully set up the options again every time. Surely, there must be a way of backing up these options.

So, I searched the Internet to find such a system, and came up with some functions, produced by digwp.com. Their functions, which were for adding to the functions.php file, were themselves based on a plugin called "Gantry Export and Import Options" by Hassan Derakhshandeh. Once more, we see how many people are using each others' code! The version I used was at https://digwp.com/2014/04/backup-restore-theme-options/, but I needed to tweak it slightly.

Here is the section to save options, in full.

```
1143: /* Section to save options */
1144: /*
1145: Backup/Restore Theme Options
1146: @ https://digwp.com/2014/04/backup-
restore-theme-options/
1147: Go to "Appearance > Backup Options" to
export/import theme settings
1148: (based on "Gantry Export and Import
Options" by Hassan Derakhshandeh)
1149:
1150: I (OCWS) have edited the code slightly, so
that it works with Child Themes
1151:
1152: Usage:
```

```
1153:   1. Add entire backup/restore snippet to
functions.php
  1154:
  1155: */
  1156: class backup_restore_theme_options {
  1157:
  1158:  function backup_restore_theme_options() {
  1159:      add_action('admin_menu', array(&$this,
'admin_menu'));
  1160:  }
  1161:  function admin_menu() {
  1162:      //  add_submenu_page($parent_slug,
$page_title, $menu_title, $capability, $menu_slug,
$function);
  1163:      //  $page =
add_submenu_page('themes.php', 'Backup Options',
'Backup Options', 'manage_options', 'backup-options',
array(&$this, 'options_page'));
  1164:
  1165:      //  add_theme_page($page_title,
$menu_title, $capability, $menu_slug, $function);
  1166:      $page = add_theme_page('Backup Options',
'Backup Options', 'manage_options', 'backup-options',
array(&$this, 'options_page'));
  1167:
  1168:      add_action("load-{$page}", array(&$this,
'import_export'));
  1169:  }
  1170:  function import_export() {
  1171:              $ocwsqt_option_name =
get_option( 'stylesheet' );
  1172:      if (isset($_GET['action']) &&
($_GET['action'] == 'download')) {
  1173:          header("Cache-Control: public,
must-revalidate");
  1174:          header("Pragma: hack");
  1175:          header("Content-Type: text/plain");
  1176:          header('Content-Disposition:
attachment; filename="'.$ocwsqt_option_name.'-
options-'.date("dMy").'.dat"');
  1177:          echo serialize($this-
>_get_options());
  1178:          die();
  1179:      }
```

```
1180:     if (isset($_POST['upload']) &&
check_admin_referer('shapeSpace_restoreOptions',
'shapeSpace_restoreOptions')) {
1181:         if ($_FILES["file"]["error"] > 0) {
1182:         // error
1183:         } else {
1184:         $options =
unserialize(file_get_contents($_FILES["file"]["tmp_
name"]));
1185:         if ($options) {
1186:             foreach ($options as $option)
{
1187:                 update_option($option-
>option_name, unserialize($option->option_value));
1188:             }
1189:         }
1190:     }
1191:
    wp_redirect(admin_url('themes.php?page=backup-
options'));
1192:         exit;
1193:     }
1194: }
1195: function options_page() { ?>
1196:
1197:     <div class="wrap">
1198:         <?php screen_icon(); ?>
1199:         <h2>Backup/Restore  Theme
Options</h2>
1200:         <form  action=""  method="POST"
enctype="multipart/form-data">
1201:             <style>#backup-options td {
display: block; margin-bottom: 20px; }</style>
1202:             <table id="backup-options">
1203:             <tr>
1204:                 <td>
1205:                     <h3>Backup/Export</h3>
1206:                     <p>Here are the stored
settings for the current theme:</p>
1207:                     <p><textarea
class="widefat  code"  rows="20"  cols="100"
onclick="this.select()"><?php echo serialize($this-
>_get_options()); ?></textarea></p>
1208:                     <p><a
href="?page=backup-options&action=download"
class="button-secondary">Download as file</a></p>
```

```
1209:                    </td>
1210:                    <td>
1211:                        <h3>Restore/Import</h3>
1212:                        <p><label
class="description" for="upload">Restore a previous
backup</label></p>
1213:                        <p><input type="file"
name="file" /> <input type="submit" name="upload"
id="upload" class="button-primary" value="Upload
file" /></p>
1214:                        <?php if
(function_exists('wp_nonce_field'))
wp_nonce_field('shapeSpace_restoreOptions',
'shapeSpace_restoreOptions'); ?>
1215:                    </td>
1216:                </tr>
1217:              </table>
1218:          </form>
1219:      </div>
1220:
1221:  <?php }
1222:  function _display_options() {
1223:      $options = unserialize($this-
>_get_options());
1224:  }
1225:  function _get_options() {
1226:      global $wpdb;
1227:
1228:                    $ocwsqt_option_name =
get_option( 'stylesheet' );
1229:
1230:      return $wpdb->get_results("SELECT
option_name, option_value FROM {$wpdb->options}
WHERE option_name = '".$ocwsqt_option_name."'");
1231:  }
1232:  }
1233:  new backup_restore_theme_options();
1234:  /* End of options saving section */
```

I added the changes at lines 1171, 1228 and 1230, which you won't find in the original version on the digwp.com page quoted. These amendments were necessary, so that the backup system now works for Child Themes, as well as the Parent Theme.

And that fact leads me on to the next chapter. Although I

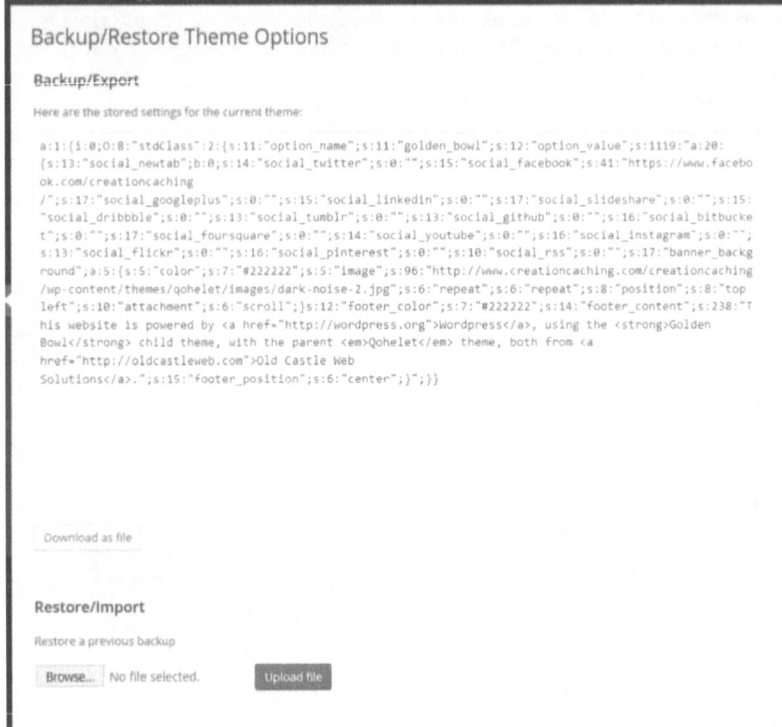

am pleased with the Qohelet theme, I did not want to tweak it further. I wanted site specific changes to be made by a child theme, so that Qohelet has a much more general purpose use.

Golden Bowl Child Theme

It is good practise to use child themes. If using a third party theme, then, if this theme gets updated, the amendments in the child theme are not lost. It seemed sensible to me to use this practise, which has become my norm, even though the parent theme was my own. I anticipate that I will make many other websites, using the Qohelet theme. I want to make these site specific, but still enable a single

update for the original Qohelet theme to cascade to all necessary sites. The obvious answer is to make use of child themes. So Golden Bowl was born.

Like with a normal theme, the main file for a child theme is style.css. But notice the early lines of code.

File style.css

```
001: /*
002: Theme Name:      Golden Bowl
003: Theme URI:       http://oldcastleweb.com
004: Description:     This child theme has been
developed for the Creation Caching website. It is
based on the Qohelet theme, which was built by Old
Castle Web Solutions.
```

```
005: Author:          Old Castle Web Solutions
006: Author URI:      http://oldcastleweb.com
007: Template:        qohelet
008: Version:         0.1
009: GitHub  Theme  URI:
https://github.com/pftaylor61/golden_bowl
010: GitHub Branch:     master
011: */
012:
013: @import url("../qohelet/style.css");
```

The lines to notice are the Template line, where it is
specified that we are adapting the qohelet theme. This
matches the Text Domain line in the Qohelet style.css. Also,
notice line 13. This requires the application to use the Qohelet
style.css for all its styles, except for the ones added to this new
child theme's file. So, we do not need to redo all the styles. We
just copy any that we want to amend, and add any new ones
that we might need.

My main changes are shown below:

```
018: body {
019:       background-color: #566D7E;
020:          background-image:
url(./images/thbg.png);
021:       background-repeat: repeat-x;
022:       background-position: top;
023: }
024:
025: #maincontentcontainer {
026:         clear: both;
027:   width: 90%;
028:       margin-left:auto;
029:       margin-right:auto;
030:       background-color:#ececec;
031: }
032:
033: #bannercontainer {
```

```
034:          clear: both;
035:     width: 90%;
036:          margin-left:auto;
037:          margin-right:auto;
038:
039: }
```

In the body, I have altered the background color. Then I created a thin background image, which I have set to repeat horizontally (x) but not vertically (y). This background image just makes a nice gradient from a darker color blending to the lighter color, already defined as the background color. This produces a nice gradient effect at the top of a page, and simply continues down the page at the same constant color that the image finishes with.

The next big change is that the main content container is set to 90%, instead of 100% (which is how Qohelet has it). The margin settings force this to the center, so that the remaining page has a 5% margin on both sides. The banner container is restricted in the same way.

This effect looks nice on large screens, but is not suitable for a smartphone screen. So I needed to add a media query, to ensure that these two sections return to 100% width for small screens.

```
041: @media screen and (max-width: 650px) {
042:     #maincontentcontainer {
043:          clear: both;
044:          width: 100%;
045:          background-color:#ececec;
046:     }
```

```
047:
048:        #bannercontainer {
049:                clear: both;
050:                width: 100%;
051:        }
052:
053: }
```

The other changes in Golden Bowl's style.css are all minor changes of color, font size etc.

Other Files

If other files are added to the child theme, they completely replace their counterpart in the parent theme (the exception to this is functions.php - more on that later).

I only wanted a tiny change to footer.php, but the whole file has to be replaced. Therefore, I just copied the entire footer.php file, then added just one tiny change, to the <footer> section, as shown:

```
        <footer  class="site-footer  row"
role="contentinfo">
                <div id="ocwsgb_sponsors">
                    <h3>Our Sponsors</h3>
                </div>
```

This change is simply because I wanted the footer "sidebar" widgets to be all about the site's sponsors.

I have already mentioned the small change made in the header, but I will repeat it here. Once again, the entire header.php file had to be copied. Then I amended the banner container section, thus:

```
<div id="bannercontainer">
   <div class="banner row">
      <?php if ( is_front_page() ) {
                                    echo
ocwssl_function('ocwssl_thin');

      } ?>
   </div> <!-- /.banner.row -->
</div> <!-- /#bannercontainer --
```

This is the code that produces the slider on the front page. It is the if (is_front_page()) test that determines if the front page is in view.

The exception to the replacement rule is functions.php. New functions can be added to the child theme's functions.php, which don't appear in the parent theme. If a function appears in both files, then the application preferentially uses the child theme, so it is basically a replacement function. But there is no need to copy all the other functions. They will work as already defined.

Golden Bowl only needed two new functions in the functions.php file.

```
22: if ( ! function_exists( 'qohelet_get_credits'
) ) {
23:    function qohelet_get_credits() {
24:        $output = '';
25:        /*
26:                $output = sprintf( '%1$s <a
href="%2$s" title="%3$s">%4$s</a>',
27:            esc_html__( 'Proudly powered by',
'qohelet' ),
28:            esc_url( esc_html__(
'http://wordpress.org/', 'qohelet' ) ),
```

```
29:              esc_attr( esc_html__( 'Semantic
Personal Publishing Platform', 'qohelet' ) ),
30:              esc_html__( 'WordPress', 'qohelet' )
31:        );
32:                      * The code belw needs
amending for translation purposes
33:                          */
34:                  $output = 'This website is
powered by <a
href="http://wordpress.org">Wordpress</a>, using
the <strong>Golden Bowl</strong> child theme, with
the parent <em>Qohelet</em> theme, both from <a
href="http://oldcastleweb.com">Old Castle Web
Solutions</a>.';
35:
36:        return $output;
37:    }
38: }
39:
40:  add_action('after_setup_theme',
'remove_admin_bar');
41:
42: function remove_admin_bar() {
43: if (!current_user_can('administrator') &&
!is_admin()) {
44:    show_admin_bar(false);
45: }
46: }
```

I probably didn't need the "if" test in 22, but I included it just in case. This function just alters the credits published at the bottom of the page.

The second function means that the admin bar is not seen, if the current logged in user is not an administrator. This function is applied, by the hook in line 40.

Other Plugins

Most Wordpress sites need a number of other plugins. This chapter lists the ones that I have used, explaining what they do, and where they are from.

We will start with some other plugins that I had previously made.

OCWS Admin Bar

This is really just for the convenience of the administrator. It changes the application logo at the top left to that of Old Castle Web Services. It also adds a convenient new dropdown menu, to get access to useful sections of the oldcastleweb.com site. On the front end, the administrator's admin bar will allow the user easy access to plugins, as well as themes. Note that my Golden Bowl theme has already removed the front end admin bar from non-administrators.

OCWS Admin Bar Greeting

This simple plugin is because of a Wordpress irritant. By default, the greeting at the top right of the admin bar says "Howdy...". That irritates me! This plugin changes that to "Welcome...". In fact, an admin UI allows any alternative greeting to be used. All OCWS plugins and themes are available for download, from http://www.oldcastleweb.com

Akismet

Akismet, from Automattic, the creators of Wordpress, is a very reliable anti-spam plugin. Get it from http://automattic.com/wordpress-plugins/

All in One Favicon

This makes it easy to define your own favicons. In fact, I define a different favicon for front and back ends. I like the back end favicon to be the sane OCWS castle logo. https://wordpress.org/plugins/all-in-one-favicon/

Capability Manager Enhanced

From https://wordpress.org/plugins/capability-manager-enhanced/

This useful plugin makes it easy to define new user roles. Then the roles can be edited. I wanted a role that just allowed access to making comments. This was the subscriber role. I then created subscriber plus, which added only one new capability - the capability to create and edit creation caches. The use of this plugin meant a careful amendment to the Creation Cache Custom Post Type, to make capability editing of Creation Caches possible.

Download Manager

From Shaon, https://wordpress.org/plugins/download-manager/

This plugin allows files to be uploaded, categorized and labelled. These can then be placed as download links in any page or post, using specially generated shortcodes.

Github Updater

Many Wordpress plugins and themes are now kept on Github, instead of the tediously slow Wordpress repository. This plugin allows Github-hosted plugins easily to be updated, as if they were on Wordpress. Although I don't have any yet, this updater also works for plugins and themes hosted at Bitbucket. https://github.com/afragen/github-updater

Github Link

This is a fun plugin. It just places a little icon next to each plugin, so that you can see at a glance whether they are hosted at Wordpress, Github or Bitbucket.

Image Widget

From Modern Tribe: https://wordpress.org/plugins/image-widget/

There are lots of image widgets out there. I even tried making my own. But this is better, and it is free.

Login Logo

This enables the login page to be amended, using your own logo, instead of that of Wordpress. This gives a more professional branded look, if you are allowing users to log in to your site. https://wordpress.org/plugins/login-logo/

Simple Wordpress Membership

This allows really good control of your membership system. It allows the use of a payment gateway, such as PayPal, to restrict access to certain membership levels. Thus, my Subscriber Plus level, allowing the creation and editing of Creation Caches, requires a $20 annual fee. https://wordpress.org/plugins/simple-membership/

These are the only plugins necessary for the Creation Caching website. A couple of others were added for development purposes, but were removed, when no longer needed.

Adding the Static Pages

At this point, all the programming was done. Now it was a matter of testing, and testing, and adding some static content.

Some static content was needed, as a result of decisions I had made earlier. For example, the Membership plugin that I had added required a few pages to be created, or edited; pages for registration, logging in, resetting passwords, viewing profiles etc.

Then I wanted a whole menu of information, to help people understand the Creation cache concept. Pages were created to explain creation caching, and its predecessors, as well as ideas on how to make a cache, and how to hide it. Some pdfs were made of some of this information, so the Download Manager plugin was used to organize links for these to be downloaded tidily.

A menu was needed for the Creation Caches themselves. This links to the archive page for the caches.

Finally, room was left for a blog. This blog will enable there to be news for the Creation Caching community.

All of these pages had to be organized into a menu. The menu options in Wordpress can be found from Appearance > Menu. I always find it important to craft the menu carefully and exactly, rather than leave Wordpress to organize the listings itself.

Testing

I have done more testing on this site than any previous site that I have made. It was tested over and over again, as an admin, then using dummy registered names under Subscriber and Subscriber Plus levels, to check whether I could access the comments and creation cache systems with those capabilities or not. And all the time the testing was going on, I had a responsive landing page on the actual domain, rather than allowing the public near the real site, which was still being tested.

Launch

Ahead of time, I had planned a launch date of January 15th 2016, together with a Facebook page. It was frustrating to wait, because I thought I had the site ready weeks before, but in the week approaching the launch date, new problems arose, which required minor adjustments to some of the coding. It would seem to me that it is better to have a long reach launch date, and to do the extensive testing in advance, so that everything works perfectly, as it should.

What Next?

I have no doubt that, once the site is being used, teething problems will arise. And there are some big things that could go wrong. The biggest sets of coding are the Creation Cache plugin, and the Qohelet theme. It seems to me that both of these have a life beyond the Creation Caching website. There are several useful code snippets and functions from both that can be reused elsewhere. The Qohelet theme, in particular, is now set to become the foundation stone of my design of other websites. Meanwhile, the Creation Cache plugin has taught be some of the pitfalls of big PHP design, as well as the advantages of splitting the project into smaller, more manageable, more achievable parts, so that the plugin gradually evolves from the pieces! And that piece of unfortunate evolutionary propaganda is probably the best place to end this account of a major web design journey.

Appendix 1: Web Development Books

There are lots of good books that I could recommend, to help you with the task of designing a site like this. But I am going to recommend just two.

Web Programming Step by Step

http://www.lulu.com/shop/jessica-miller-and-victoria-kirst-and-marty-stepp/web-programming-step-by-step-2nd-edition/paperback/product-20293270.html

The most important background textbook is this mammoth work, by Miller, Kirst, and Stepp. You won't find it in the bookshops. You need to order it from Lulu. It assumes nothing. It takes you from basic knowledge of HTML, through CSS, Javascript, PHP, Jquery, SQL and Ajax. Any web developer needs this book in his / her armory, in my opinion. However, it does not give specific details on Wordpress, so you also need:

Professional Wordpress Plugin Development

By Williams, Richard, and Tadlock.

This book can be bought in most places, but is probably easiest to get from

Amazon. The book goes through in detail the technologies required to produce plugins, and gives examples bit by bit. If you examine the code in the Creation Cache plugin carefully, you will see that I have been able to use a lot of their code.

Appendix 2: Old Castle Web Solutions

All of my web development work is carried out under the

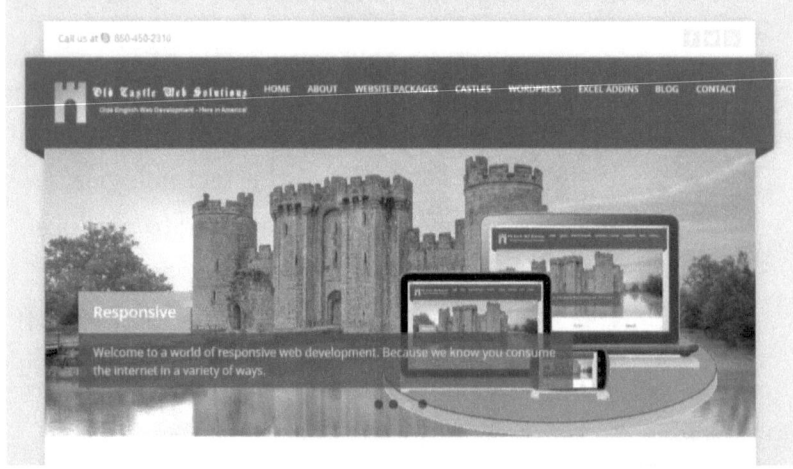

banner of Old Castle Web Solutions. This website, at oldcastleweb.com, will explain to you how I go about producing a Wordpress based site, and what costs you can expect for it. Because costs can vary, I recommend that you look at the website for the latest details. At the time of publication, a basic, simple web application can be yours for about $400.

All of my plugins and themes are to be found listed on this website. The code for all of these is held at Github, which is a social coding site - that is to say, it encourages and facilitates community sharing of code, and collaborative efforts. At the present time, all my plugins and themes are open source and free. Because I have made use of so many other people's code in my own coding, I would feel a bit awkward about charging. Basically, I want to be able to give back to the community of coders, from which I have benefited so much.

Old Castle Web Solutions

The new book from Paul Taylor is an easy-to-follow handbook to Presuppositional Apologetics. It covers topics on how Jesus defended the faith, how Peter, Paul and Jude defended the faith, and how the Bible speaks to unbelievers.

When Jesus spoke words of comfort to Jairus in Mark 5, He could have offered all sorts of evidence, to enable Jairus to believe. Yet the evidence was already available. Instead, Jesus gave the important context, in which all the evidence is to be interpreted - Only Believe.

Available from Amazon, Mount St Helens Creation Center (mshcreationcenter.org), and wherever books are sold.

Where Birds Eat Horses helps you spot the pseudo-scientific language used by evolutionists. The subtitle is "The Language of Evolution", and the book shows how the "evidence" for evolution consists not in scientific experiment, but in the clever and deceptive use of language. Learn how to spot fuzzy words, magic words, and false presuppositions.

"Paul has penned yet another stellar defense of the biblical account of creation. You must have this book!" **Carl Gallups**

"Paul Taylor is uniquely gifted with insight into this groundless and godless philosophy. May God use this book to equip millions." **Ray Comfort**

Available from Amazon, Mount St Helens Creation Center (mshcreationcenter.org), and wherever books are sold.

Doctrine is not something that is cold. It should be alive and vibrant. It is relevant, because it links the teaching of the Bible to everyday situations.

Most Christian doctrines are based on a foundation of Genesis. Paul Taylor has taken some of those teachings that matter to us most - the Trinity, the Deity of Christ, the Inerrancy of Scripture, Sin and Death, Salvation, Faith and Abraham and the Second Coming. In an easy to follow style, he looks at what the Bible says about each teaching, and then shows that it is much easier to understand and accept each teaching, when we start by believing the early chapters of Genesis to be true.

Itching Ears

How the most important Christian doctrines are rooted in Genesis

Paul F Taylor

Available from Amazon, Mount St Helens Creation Center (mshcreationcenter.org), and wherever books are sold.

The two epistles to the Thessalonians contain much of the basic, biblical teaching on the End Times. For this reason, they have often been controversial. Yet the material they contain is essential for anyone who wants to get to grips with this subject, as well as providing an insight into the establishment of a church, which the apostle Paul commends as behaving exactly as a church should.

Paul Taylor argues that a literal reading of these epistles leads one to a Historic (Posttribulation) Premillennial understanding of the End Times.

Available from Amazon, Mount St Helens Creation Center (mshcreationcenter.org), and wherever books are sold.